# Life in all its fullness

## PHILIP POTTER

WILLIAM B. EERDMANS
PUBLISHING COMPANY
GRAND RAPIDS, MICHIGAN

This American edition published 1982 through special arrangement with
the World Council of Churches by Wm. B. Eerdmans Publishing
Company, 255 Jefferson Ave. S.E., Grand Rapids, Michigan, 49503

**Library of Congress Cataloging in Publication Data**

Potter, Philip.
  Life in all its fullness.

    1. Christian life — 1960-    — Addresses, essays,
lectures.  2. Ecumenical movement — Addresses, essays,
lectures.  3. World Council of Churches — Addresses,
essays, lectures.  I. Title.
BV4501.2.P557  1982    248.4    82-5079
ISBN 0-8028-1938-9     AACR2

# Contents

# Preface

For several years friends and colleagues have vainly been trying to persuade me to publish my writings and speeches, or more ambitiously to write books on subjects which have been at the heart of my ministry. I have stubbornly ignored these pleas, for three reasons.

First, when I started my ministry in 1948, there was plenty of theological writing by the giants of the time — Barth, Brunner, Bultmann, Dodd, Manson, the Niebuhrs, the Baillies, Tillich, to name only a few. Some of us who got engaged in the ecumenical movement made a clear decision that we would devote ourselves to working out strategies and programmes and to labouring for the unity, renewal, witness, and service of the church. Speaking, yes; writing addresses and short articles, yes; but producing books... well, there were enough of those around. Second, my early training was in a law office and in the law court, and that meant preparing concise briefs, knowing where to find the legal references, and participating in the effort of convincing witnesses, judge, and jury. My later training for the ministry only fortified this preference of oral to written advocacy. Third, my life during these more than thirty years has been mainly on the frontier with youth, students, and people involved in the mission and service of the church in encounter with the hard realities of our tempestuous world. Events have moved so quickly and have been so pressing and controversial that practically all my energies have been spent in posing and seeking to answer concretely the question: What is to be done?

Now, in my sixtieth year, some of my friends and colleagues have decided to take the matter in hand. Thanks to the efforts of my deceased wife Doreen and of my former assistant Machteld van Vredenburch in collecting my speeches and writings, and of Ans van der Bent, the librarian of the World Council of Churches, in bringing all this material together, an attempt has been made to select a number of them for publication. By a happy circumstance Marc Reuver, until recently director of IDOC (the International Documentation Service based in Rome), has taken up residence in Geneva and agreed to undertake this almost impossible task. He has gone through boxes of papers, many of them in incomplete form, and has woven a number of them together in a remarkably coherent pattern. He has brought to this task the vast knowledge and skill of one accustomed to editing varied documents. He has accomplished his work with the enthusiasm and sympathy of a fellow pilgrim on the ecumenical way, and I want to record my immense gratitude to him.

All the material in this book has its origin in my work with the World Council of Churches since 1967, first as director of the Commission on World Mission and Evangelism and later as General Secretary. A wide variety of concerns which form the ecumenical agenda has been treated in sermons and addresses all over the world. If there is a dominating theme it is that indicated by the title, *Life in all its Fullness*. Here I would like to indicate two threads which have been used to weave my convictions together.

First, the Bible has played a central role in my life and thought. At the age of sixteen, when I became a lay preacher, I began to read John Wesley's sermons and especially the preface to those sermons. There he said, in the words of St. Thomas Aquinas, quoted by Jeremy Taylor in his *Holy Living and Holy Dying*, that he desired to be *homo unius libri*, a man of one book — the Bible. That became my motto. Wesley was one of the best read men of the eighteenth century and in many languages, but the Scriptures, together with prayer and the Lord's Supper, were for him the means of grace. All the words of writers were brought into dialogue with the word of God in the Bible and this was for him the way of doing theology. Moreover, theology was for the sake of evangelism, the proclamation in word and deed of the gospel of the kingdom of God in all the dimensions of our human existence.

Later, in the Student Christian Movement, I learned, particularly through the writings and teaching of Suzanne de Dietrich (significantly her academic training was not in theology but electrical engineering), the centrality of Bible study for confronting courageously the issues of doubt and faith, and of all the intellectual disciplines as they impinge on our total existence as persons called to witness in the world with the "costly grace" of God. We were taught to have the Bible in one hand and the newspaper in the other. Without the newspapers, symbolizing our daily human and global reality, the Bible seems remote and irrelevant. Without the Bible, the baffling and often sordid and tragic events of our time are meaningless. So while I have been an avid reader in many fields, it is the study of the Bible and of biblical theology which has been my main sustenance.

Second, as a Caribbean person containing in myself many cultures, I am fascinated by the call to dialogue, the encounter of life with life, and especially the dialogue of cultures. I have been personally enriched in my faith and life by my reading of the literature of many cultures and above all by my encounter with people of all walks of life in many parts of the world. There is a tendency nowadays to regard the meeting of cultures, including theologies, as a source of division and conflict. I have discovered that with humility, imagination, humour, and courage, this meeting of cultures is in fact the only hope for humankind to attain fullness of life in all its shared diversity in the Christ who contains and holds all things together.

Here I owe much to the words of the apostles Peter and Paul in their encyclical letters to the churches of Asia Minor. Peter exhorts: "As each has received a gift, employ it for one another, as good stewards of God's varied, multi-form grace" (1 Pet. 4:10). Similarly Paul testifies: "To me, though I am the very least of all the saints, this grace was given, to preach to the Gentiles the unsearchable riches of Christ, and to make all see what is the plan of the mystery hidden for ages in God who created all things; that through the church the varied, multi-form wisdom of God might now be made known to the principalities and powers in the heavenly places" (Eph. 3:8-10). God's grace and wisdom are manifested in varied forms through the Body of Christ in the body politic, with all its varied cultures and challenges. The future of the ecumenical movement, and of what we now call the conciliar fellowship of the churches in each place and in all places, depends on our engaging boldly and joyously in this dialogue of cultures as expressed in the life, thinking, and witness of the people of God among the peoples of the world.

This collection of writings is dedicated to the memory of my wife Doreen, who was not only a creative companion for nearly twenty-five years, but was in constant dialogue with me about what I said and wrote and, further, corrected and typed nearly all my writings. The last chapter in this book, "A Growing Community of Faith," which is taken from my address to the Central Committee of the World Council of Church nearly two months after her death last year, is a fitting tribute to her and to all she shared with me.

Geneva, July 1981                              *Philip Potter*

# 1. Seeking a Saviour

Jesus saves!

The words come easily for many Christians. Indeed, they sometimes come too easily. The idea is widespread that the world needs something we have to give and is waiting with bated breath to hear what we have to say — a "word from the Lord." But the common notion of much popular piety that Jesus saves our souls does not find all that ready an audience in the world today. The world does not in fact appear to be looking for a Saviour in that sense; nor does it seem to be asking the question King Zedekiah once put to Jeremiah: "Is there any word from the Lord?" (Jer. 37:17).

"Salvation" can become a religious slogan, understandable only to an in-group, when we lose sight of the biblical roots of the word "to save." The Hebrew verb *yasha*, to save — from which the name Jesus, "he who saves," is derived — was a thoroughly this-worldly word. It meant "to be wide, to be spacious." Its opposite was *sara*, "to be narrow" — whether physically, intellectually, or spiritually. From this figure of width and spaciousness, the word *yasha* came to be used for rescuing people from danger or misfortune, gaining victory in battle, and liberating those who were confined. The Psalmist even described the very creation of the world in terms of God's working *salvation* by liberating, through his word and Spirit, formless matter into order, giving freedom to creation and people to be themselves (Ps. 74:12-17).

Unfortunately, when this Hebrew word was translated into Greek, *soteria* was used. *Soteria* for the Greeks spoke of deliverance from bodily life, rescue from the burden of material existence. This is quite contrary to the Hebrew understanding of salvation as being *for* the world rather than *from* the world. And too often in the history of Christianity it has been the Greek idea which has predominated over the Hebrew one.

Can this Hebrew idea of salvation *for* the world find a hearing today? Are our world and its inhabitants, the nations, races, cultures, and religions, "narrow," sick, weak, in bondage, looking to be liberated and healed? In this sense the answer seems clear: the world *is* in search of a Saviour.

We must look more closely at some facets of the biblical idea of salvation and at the Saviour whom the Bible proclaims.

*No empty glory*

The God who created the world by liberating it from chaos sends his only Son in the flesh and blood of human beings. In a world of sin and bondage and death, Jesus is the one who frees, who makes life wide and spacious. The sick and demon-possessed are healed with the words, "Your faith has saved you...." The tax-collector Zacchaeus, a hated outcast among his own people because he collaborated with the colonial power to squeeze them economically, is told by this Jesus, "Today is salvation come to your house."

When the Apostle Paul became a man in Christ, liberated by this same Jesus, he gained a new discernment of how people are caught in self-destroying ambiguities and perversities which prevent them from being free in themselves and for others. Their cry is his own: "O wretched man that I am. Who will deliver me from the body of this death?" (Rom. 7:24). He sees that the human predicament is that of the whole of creation, which is writhing in pain, waiting eagerly to be released from the fate of nothingness, waiting for the revealing of the free sons of God. To humanity and to creation Paul proclaims that the gospel is the power of God for salvation, freedom.

Paul deals with this issue in a remarkable way in his letter to the Philippians. The Christians of Philippi were splendid people. Keen, loyal, generous, they evoked the most lovely letter we have from Paul's pen. Yet the apostle cites serious dangers in that community: they were contentious and conceited. They thought themselves better than others. They were very much concerned about their own interests and not those of others (Phil. 2:1-13).

In a word, the Philippians were self-centred. Their salvation they conceived as the freedom to assert themselves and their rights over against one another and other communities. They had not realized that being liberated from their former narrow existence should make their life wide and spacious, not exclusive but inclusive. Made free by God and for God, they should be made free for others. The German philosopher Karl Jaspers, reflecting on the tragic disaster of his country under Nazi ideology, observed that "no man is free who does not work for the freedom of others." The problem Paul lifts up to the attention of the Philippian Christians is precisely that of our sick and restricting societies today — not to mention our churches, which too often reflect society's malady of being self-enclosed.

Paul's language fits in well with contemporary psychological insights. He tells us that persons and peoples clogged up in themselves end up with emptiness. "Empty glory" means glory which eventually turns into meaninglessness. The Greeks spoke of one caught up in one's self and one's own as *idios* — the source of our word "idiot." "Each man for himself and the devil take the hindmost" is a familiar summary of the philosophy of the survival of the fittest, which still reigns in our world. George Macleod of Iona puts it more correctly: "Each man for himself and the devil take the lot."

Around the time Paul was in Rome writing this letter, an astute observer saw clearly that the mighty Roman Empire would not survive because, said he, "there is no associated enthusiasm of all." How could there be, in a world of exploited slaves and what the Romans called barbarians, of conquered peoples, and of conspicuous wealth for a few? The words of the economist John Kenneth Galbraith about contemporary America accurately describe the situation in the Roman Empire: "public poverty in the midst of private affluence."

What Paul is saying is that people may be saved, liberated, healed from their personal and corporate self-regard. Their narrow self-conceit and self-interest can give way to being free for others, free to be with others in mutual respect and concern. He invites the Philippians and us to fix our gaze on Christ the Saviour, the true liberator.

Paul goes on to reflect on his own encounter with Christ. What transformed his life was the form and content of the salvation Christ offered. How did Christ become his Saviour and the Saviour of all? How has he freed us from ourselves? Precisely by being and doing the complete opposite to what we are and do.

First, Christ did not seek to rival God or assert his equality with him. To do so is the fundamental human tendency. The Bible shrewdly mirrors this human trait in its accounts of Adam and Eve, Cain and Abel, and the Tower of Babel. Once Adam and Eve fell for the offer of the serpent to make them like God, they were no longer able to respond to God for themselves and for others. They became part of creation rather than master of it. Their freedom was gone, and they had no response to the question, "Where are you?" Their son Cain had only a counter-question when God asked where his slain brother was: "Am I my brother's keeper?" The human story unfolds further with men seeking to build their cities and empires. The symbol of the Tower of Babel tells us that their great motive was "let us make a name for ourselves." The existentialist writer Jean-Paul Sartre put all this succinctly: "To be a man means to be God.... Human reality is a pure effort to become God."

But when we turn to Christ, says Paul, we find that he wanted no empty glory. He did not wish to assert his Godhead over against God, thus ending in emptiness, nothingness. Rather he emptied himself, taking on the same form or structure as the Greek girl whom Paul and Silas had cured in Philippi (Acts 16:16-18) — a slave. He would be no Greek or Roman saviour or hero at the head of conquering armies and claiming divine honours. He became a man, completely exposed to people, completely at their disposal, exploitable by them, because he allowed himself to be completely at God's disposal, his slave.

Second, this Jesus sought not his own interests but those of God and therefore of humanity. Here is the paradox: Jesus freely accepted this restricted and apparently narrow life of man as a servant, even a slave, ending in death on the cross; and yet it is by this means that he is fully revealed for what he is, Lord and Saviour. He becomes and is shown to be what he in fact is, not by self-assertion but by his dependence on God's purpose and his self-giving for humanity.

Paul describes how in turning to Christ he found that all his racial, social, and religious baggage was worthless. His only plus was Christ: "For me, to live is Christ" (Phil. 1:21). He became himself as he gave up being self-centred and self-enclosed. Becoming himself, he became like Christ a man for others. And so Paul says to the Philippians and to us, "You become truly yourselves, real men and women, only as you renounce any confidence in your own view of yourselves and in your rights and interests, and only as you commit yourselves wholly to the realities which lie beyond yourselves — God your Creator and your fellow creatures."

Therefore, declares Paul, keep on working out the salvation you have already received, but do this "with fear and trembling" (Phil. 2:12) — an attitude opposed to the Philippians' self-conceit and self-confidence. The constant threat we humans face is lapsing into self-centredness. Paul reminds us of our dependence on one another. It is with fear and trembling that we work out our freedom because, like Christ, we rely completely on God. All is of God. Our will, our work, our capacity to make decisions, our ability to put them into practice — in short, all that makes us human is from God and destined for God.

What are the consequences of taking this conception of ourselves and our task seriously? First of all, we must be clear that we can never be effective instruments for the gospel of salvation unless the work of salvation is going on in us, unless we are being liberated, individually and corporately, in Christ and for Christ. Paul's words turn the searchlight squarely on self-regarding church structures concerned mainly about extending their own interest. "Structure" is a Latinized equivalent of a word Paul uses in describing Christ: the form (or structure) — *morphé* — of God, of a servant. Are we willing as churches that our institutions, our traditions, our structures be broken by God, that we become completely humbled in order to be the serving people of God? Or when we call for renewal of our institutions and structures do we really mean bringing them up-to-date so that they can survive and maintain some strength?

Second, the salvation, the liberation which Christ offers and we must keep on working out takes us out of the narrow confines of racial, social, national, and denominational selfishness and exclusiveness. Paul calls on the whole Christian community to have "the same mind, having the same love, becoming in full accord and of one mind" (Phil. 2:2). Christian churches have, through the ecumenical movement, been moving from cooperation to joint action for mission, though rather slowly. But unity in life and action depends on our willingness to be liberated from our selfish structures. Pope John XXIII saw this clearly when he called the massive, monolithic, exclusive, and excluding Roman Catholic Church to renewal of its form and structures. He realized with the apostle that only when we are thus being liberated can we share a common life in humble service of humankind.

Third, the attitude of messengers of freedom who are being saved must be one of self-giving and concern for others. Paul prays that the Philippians may grow more and more in love with knowledge and discernment (Phil. 1:9). Love which is disciplined by discernment and knowledge enables us to put aside our preconceived ideas and opens us to understand the situation of other people. This is the way of dialogue, the seeing eyes and ears of love, whether with persons of other faiths or with persons of no faith. It is an openness to others which enables God to be at work in us, both to will and to do his good pleasure. This attitude is including, not excluding. All human concerns — the longing for liberation from racial and social discrimination and for a just life in a shared community — are our concern. Our love, our servant life, must be deployed in every way available for their salvation, their freedom. Development projects, struggles against imperialistic and interventionist wars, solidarity with the poor and oppressed, the fight for racial and social equality — all these are signs of the salvation we are called ceaselessly to work out. The sole criterion is that in them all the Saviour becomes visible in word and deed.

Finally, salvation, the liberation which Christ offers, has a goal. We are saved, freed for the future — the commonwealth or common life together in the unveiled presence of God (Phil. 3:20). With our hope steadily before us we are given the power to forget what is behind us, even our glorious tradition, and press on to our high calling in Christ. Our hope, our plans, our work are all of God. Human aspirations and strategies and efforts for a true commonwealth must be turned towards their true source — God, whose structure or form is the servant Christ for us. Our task is to help this turning towards God and his commonwealth.

*Continuing in the word*

To orient and guide us in working out our salvation we do indeed have a "word from the Lord." But just as we go wrong when we understand and proclaim salvation as if it were merely a cure for the soul, we err if we view the word of God as a quick spiritual fix, a magic religious formula, a ready-made, easy-to-use, once-for-all divine answer to all our questions.

There was a word from the Lord to the beleaguered kingdom of Judah in Zedekiah's time (Jer. 37:17). Like many other prophets, Jeremiah had spoken it without compromise — and the king had surely heard it even before he asked the prophet about it.

The word from the Lord which Judah needed to hear — and we today no less — was a thundering denunciation of injustice. The purpose of the existence of God's people was to reflect the character of their God, whose name is "the Lord, our righteousness." They were not to be unjust, to oppress the alien and the fatherless and the widow, or to shed innocent blood. Jeremiah attacked the ardour of their excessive concern for national identity and religious institutions. Instead, the people were to seek the peace — the well-being, the total reintegration of life — of the city into which they had been sent into exile. "Pray to the Lord on its behalf," the prophet said, "for in its peace, its welfare, you will find peace, your welfare. For I know the plans I have for you, plans for peace, for welfare and not for evil, to give you a future and a hope."

Commenting on this word from the Lord, Martin Buber observes that God desires not religiousness, but a human people living together, with the makers of decisions vindicating those who thirst for justice, the strong having pity for the weak. Out of a common humanity he wills to make his kingdom.

To the Jews who believed in him, the gospel of John says, Jesus stressed the importance of *continuing* in the word

(8:31-36). As with Paul's message to the Philippians, it is this ongoing process of listening to and obeying the word of God which is at the heart of the believers' responsibility. From what Jesus said we can develop three important points about the word: its attraction; the offense it arouses; and the offer it makes.

The Jews whom Jesus addresses in John 8:31-36 had heard the debate after his announcement, "I am the light of the world; he who follows me will not walk in darkness, but will have the light of life" (8:12). They were prepared to accept him as a genuine person who spoke what was true, real, living. They were attracted by him. But that was not enough.

Many so-called secular people in our day find Jesus an attractive figure, though most would quickly add that they consider the church repugnant. Translations and paraphrases of the Bible in contemporary language are best-sellers. In the midst of the loneliness and meaninglessness of life in Western society, the search for self-understanding and fulfilment has led many people to all types of Jesus movements. The same attraction of the word may even be seen among some Marxists, who seek what they call transcendent humanism. The Marxist thinker Roger Garaudy, after reading declarations from the Second Vatican Council and the World Council of Churches, even wrote: "It may be that religion is no longer opium for the people, but yeast for the people."

But is it enough to believe Jesus, to regard him as relevant, even genuine? Jesus did not think so, and the whole gospel story is an attack on this kind of surface acceptance of him. Earlier in John's gospel, the evangelist says about such believers that "Jesus did not trust himself to them, because he knew all men and needed no one to bear witness of man; for he himself knew what was in man" (2:24-25). Jesus challenges us to go further: "If you continue in my word, you are truly my disciples, and you will know the truth, and the truth will make you free" (8:31-32).

Here we come to what we may call the offense, the scandal of the word. Truth and freedom are not external realities which can be found by human striving under the inspiration of Jesus' teaching. Truth and freedom are embodied in Jesus. Only he is true, genuine, and free. Only in communion with him, in becoming his disciples, can we receive the truth, the reality of our existence, and become really free. There is no other way.

The reaction of those Jews to this challenge was immediate: "We are descendants of Abraham, and have never been in bondage to any one" (v. 33). Relying on their historical, religious, and racial privileges, they see Jesus not as replacing their past, but as giving some further security in it. But he is challenging all that they claim to be. What is terrifying about this passage for the Christian who reads it today is that this debate is with the covenant people of God, and further with those among the covenant people who sympathized with Jesus. Here is concentrated the human predicament, which has since come to expression in many different ways. Nietzsche may have said of Jesus: "There has been only one Christian, and he died on the Cross." But Nietzsche denied the claims of Christ on his life violently, even to the point of insanity. Gandhi, who read the gospels frequently, once said to a Christian: "Jesus belongs to us all." But when asked, "And do you belong to him?", Gandhi was silent. The exclusive claim of Jesus on his life was the offense.

This is the drama of the encounter with Jesus of persons of other faiths or of none. They rely on their history, their self-understanding, their searching. They do not mind making use of the teachings of Jesus, or being inspired by him. But they cannot submit to him in faith and commitment. They judge, as the gospel puts it, *kata sarka*, according to their own understanding, according to appearances, as things have always been. They cannot face the disclosure of the truth in living form in the person of Jesus. Afraid of confronting ultimate reality, they concentrate on the temporary. They run away from the genuine and stick to what is false. They prefer the death of the past to the life of the future.

But many of us in the church are also locked into our doctrines and confessions. Our rigid traditions of the past and time-honoured practices lead us to become tools of deception, reaction, and depression. We use our traditional understanding of the faith and of the Christian ethic as a means of not facing the realities of our times. We therefore avoid the possibility of being changed, of being opened up to the future and liberated for it.

Some of us, on the other hand, would rather think of ourselves as Christian radicals. We champion movements for racial and economic justice. We favour a more contemporary ethic. We call for ecclesiastical reform to make the church more up-to-date. But like those Jews in Jesus' time who hoped that he would lead a movement of liberation against the Roman imperialists and their religious and secular collaborators, we are in danger of asserting our own conception of the truth and of seeking to secure freedom for ourselves and others by our own efforts. We are not willing to submit ourselves to the criticism of the word and to accept the way of the cross in Christ.

Jesus was relentless in characterizing the human situation — whether of orthodox or radical believers who bear the name "Christian"; or of persons of other faiths; or of agonizing secularists. "Truly, truly, I say to you, every one who commits sin is a slave of sin" (v. 34). Not to trust ourselves to Christ, not to abide in his word, is sin — no less. Luther's classic image of the sinner as a person *incurvatus in se*, bent, wrapped into himself, applies to us both individually and corporately. Whatever form our self-confidence ("we are descendants of Abraham") takes, our past determines us. We make it our own, cling to it, and try to forge our way forward on the basis of it rather than surrendering ourselves totally to Christ and his future. Therein lies the offense, the scandal of the word.

This human tragedy, which Jesus faced, and which the Reformers confronted, is still with us today. The Reformers went back to the word of God and pointed beyond the teaching of Jesus, the doctrine of the church, and the historical fact of Christendom to the very being of Christ who uncovered the reality of God and of human existence. They sharpened the scandal, the offense of the word, and directed persons to the *offer* of the word.

We are invited to listen again to Jesus' offer: "If you continue in my word, you are truly my disciples, and you will know the truth, and the truth will make you free.... If the Son makes you free, you will be free indeed" (vv. 31-32, 36). The whole drama of our salvation, our liberation, is centred in the disclosure of the reality of God in the man Jesus and in the overcoming of the offense by those who accept him in faith. That

recovery of the word for the church is what the modern movements of Christian renewal are seeking to emphasize.

How do we today receive the offer of the word which reveals
the truth and makes us free?

First, we must remain in and make our own the word, which
is Christ himself. We cannot salute Jesus, take his teachings
away, and carry on as we always have. "Faith," said Karl
Barth, "is the shattering halt in the presence of God." Here we
stop and stay. We can do no other. It is not this or that saying
of Jesus which arrests us. It is the whole of himself, the word
made flesh, full of grace and truth, the self-giving love of God,
which is the reality of our lives. As Luther put it, faith is being
*coram Deo*, before God, in the presence of him who is the light
of the world, who illumines our existence and that of the world
and gives meaning to our lives. Indeed, he becomes our life.
Gone is our own self-assertion. Gone are our securities,
including the religious and theological ones. That is the glorious
message addressed to us and to all people. That is the motive
for the church's missionary task. This message makes people
disciples of Christ, who follow him through the cross and resurrection to that endless life which gives them a totally new orientation on this life. We are turned away from ourselves, opened
to God in Christ, and therefore to the world he redeemed.

Remaining in the word also implies a willingness constantly
to be penetrated by it, questioned and changed by it. There is
no resting place for us except in Christ, who is not only yes-
terday and today but also tomorrow.

Receiving the offer of the word means, in the second place,
that we shall know the truth. That is the promise. We are all
determined by what we know — the deposit of our personal
and corporate history. We are all haunted in one way or
another by the desire to know the truth, the reality about ourselves and our world. That reality, that truth is Christ himself.
As he says earlier in this discourse in John, "You shall know
that I am" (v. 28). The truth is not a set of ideas or a programme; it is a person. And it is only in communion with him
that we become real, transparent to ourselves and to others.

But knowing him who is the truth is not only a gift, a discovery, but also an act. John's gospel makes this abundantly
clear. "He who does what is true comes to the light, that it may

be clearly seen that his deeds have been accomplished in God"
(3:21). "If any man wills to do God's will, he shall know
whether the teaching is from God..." (7:17). To know and to act
are one reality in Christian experience. Of course, such doing of
the truth is always in the perspective of what Luther called
*simul justus et peccator*. We act in faith, but we know ourselves
to be under the threat of sin. But as we abide in Christ and his
forgiving love, as we act on his word, we are enabled to go on
entering into a deeper understanding of him and of his purpose
for humanity.

Finally, such remaining in the word as leads to knowing the
truth in Christ in action will make us free. We become really
alive, open to the future which is God's promise. We are freed
from our past, freed from a false understanding of our origin
and destiny, freed from ourselves. The Jews interpreted their
relation to Abraham as a possession of the past which was for
themselves only. But the revelation to Abraham was precisely a
call to leave the past behind and to set out in faith on God's
way. Obeying that call, Abraham became the father of all the
families of the earth. The fulfilment of Abraham's act of
freedom in obedience was in Christ, who was in fact before
Abraham. The true descendants of Abraham are those who
know themselves called to exist, to step out of themselves in
faith, "ready," as Luther said, "to enter confidently into the
darkness of the future."

### Bearers of hope

When we turn to the crucified and risen Christ, we have the
joy of knowing that we are not born to die, but to enter confidently into the future in freedom and hope. This is not a matter
of accepting a dogma but an act of participating in God's
unfinished work of creation. The resurrection reveals a new and
radical freedom and hope which the Greek and Roman world
did not know. To have faith in the crucified and risen Lord is to
hope and so to join him in the work of transforming the world.
Faith — "the assurance of things hoped for, the conviction of
things not seen" (Heb. 11:1) — enables us to realize that we are
not made once for all and expected to take things as they are.

What is the nature of the hope which continuing in the word
of God offers? How can we be signs of that hope? The last

book of the Bible, the book of Revelation, give us a vision of the city, the *polis* of God — God's political future. That city is made up of all the riches of the world, for the enjoyment of all. It is an open city, excluding no one. There is freedom of movement among the peoples. All recognize themselves as bearing the name and the mark of the Lamb, the one who gave himself in love for others, who cared for others and was willing to sacrifice himself for them so that many might share God's future to the full.

Two kinds of people are excluded from this future city of God — "the cowardly, the faithless, the polluted," that is, those who refuse to commit themselves, who seek their own way, who have no hope in themselves or in others and so become corrupt; and "murderers, fornicators, sorcerers, idolaters, and all liars," that is, those who take advantage of, deceive, and deny the existence of others. The uncommitted and the exploiters exclude themselves from the life of hope.

How can we be bearers and signs of hope as we continue in the word of God? Let me briefly indicate three ways, suggested by three texts from New Testament epistles:

(1) *By giving an account of the hope which is in us.* Peter begins his letter to all the churches in Asia Minor by saying: "Blessed be the God and Father of our Lord Jesus Christ. By his great mercy we have been born anew to a living hope through the resurrection of Jesus Christ from the dead" (1 Pet. 1:3). Later he says to those who have embraced this hope: "In your hearts reverence Christ as Lord. Always be prepared to make a defense to any one who calls you to account for the hope that is in you, yet do it with gentleness and reverence." We are bearers of hope when we show to our fellow human beings the same reverence and respect that we show to Christ. The way of dialogue is the way of hope — the sharing of life with life. Remember the courtesy Jesus showed to the Samaritan woman at the well, and his acceptance of the hospitality of Zacchaeus.

(2) *By welcoming one another as Christ welcomed us* (Rom. 15:7). The whole of this Romans 15 passage is important, because it continues the discussion of chapter 14 about weak and strong Christians. The strong in this case were those who considered all meat to be clean because it was God's creation, while the weak were those who feared that eating meat which

had been dedicated to idols would contaminate their faith. So Paul says to the church in Rome: "We who are strong ought to bear with the failings of the weak, and not to please ourselves. Let each of us please his neighbour for his good, to build him up. For Christ did not please himself." Quoting from the Psalms he goes on: "For whatever was written in former days was written for our instruction, that by steadfastness and by the encouragement of the scriptures we might have hope." This is remarkable, because Paul is saying that the hope which the word of God gives is the Spirit which enables us to do what Christ did. He who was strong and rich became weak and poor for our sakes in order to build us up. Moreover, Christ welcomed us when we were outcasts, and in despair of ourselves, just as he did the woman at the well and Zacchaeus. He gave them hope. In the same way, we bring hope to others as we welcome them. We break down the barriers between Jews and Gentiles, between people of different races, sexes, classes. Welcoming others, caring for those around us, is "for the glory of God." It reveals his presence among us, the promise of the fulfilment of our hopes of living in harmony with each other in a real sharing of life with life.

(3) *By suffering with Christ.* Hope is not cheap. Our hope becomes real through the cross, the suffering and death of Christ. The dynamic of hope is self-giving love. Paul reminds us in Romans 8 that when we become children of God, calling God "Abba, Father," this gives us the freedom to be ourselves and the hope of sharing the exalted life of Christ. But there is a condition: "provided we suffer with him in order that we may also be glorified with him" (Rom. 8:17). Earlier Paul has indicated the nature of those sufferings, and how we can endure them: "We rejoice in our sufferings knowing that sufferings produce endurance, and endurance produces character, and character produces hope, and hope does not disappoint us, because God's love has been poured into our hearts through the Holy Spirit which has been given to us" (Rom. 5:3-5).

When God's love fills our hearts through the creative power of the Holy Spirit, we are free to tackle what seems impossible. We are emboldened to face all opposition. We are given the character and the capacity to endure to the very end. That is the way of hope, and it involves suffering. But in the end it is faith and hope and love which endure. And nothing can separate us from the love of Christ. That is why we can go on doing our work, the work of God's future, even when it seems difficult or impossible, because the future is God's. He has conquered in Christ. As fellow workers with him, we too shall conquer if we remain faithfully committed to this hope. That is why Paul is able to say to the church in Rome: "May the God of hope fill you with all joy and peace in believing, so that by the power of the Holy Spirit you may abound in hope" (Rom. 15:13).

# 2. Turning to freedom and fullness

We saw in the first chapter that the promise to those who continue in the word is the promise of knowing the truth which makes us free and open to others, bearers of genuine hope. This wide and inclusive understanding of salvation corresponds to the deepest longings of humanity today for togetherness and dignity, justice and peace.

But this desire for mutual respect and caring is thwarted time and again by the individual and collective selfishness of people and nations. Curiously, this frustrated search for community is seldom recognized for what it is — a profound human resistance to the call to be converted.

## Conversion in the Bible

Like "salvation," "conversion" is one of those familiar Christian words whose original biblical sense tends to be buried under layers of traditional piety. In an effort to recapture that meaning, let us try to summarize briefly what the Old and New Testaments tell us about conversion.

The most common Hebrew word used in the Old Testament to point to conversion is the verb *shub*, to turn, a familiar word which appears in its various forms more than a thousand times. (Significantly, perhaps, the noun form is hardly ever used — suggesting a corrective to our habit of freezing vital acts of commitment into theological concepts!) What do we learn from the Old Testament about this turning to which we are called?

(1) The call to turn in the Old Testament is addressed principally to God's covenant people. Israel has known first-hand the mighty acts of God in history; they have experienced who God

is and what he has done and is doing. When they turn away from him and fail to act on the basis of this knowledge and experience, when they do not live up to the covenant, they make it impossible for other nations to turn to God.

(2) The measure of the turning which is called for is God's character and his demands: it is a conversion to doing justice, practicing kindness, living with integrity, avoiding alliances with unjust states and peoples.

(3) Turning is not merely a matter of individual reorientation. It has personal and corporate dimensions. The individual is seen as a participant in a community, as someone responsible for that community and beyond. Being turned to God is also being turned to one's fellow humans. Conversion entails the service of people. This is the heart of God's law: loving the Lord above all and your neighbour as yourself. The combination of individual and social elements in the call to turn is expressed with memorable vividness by the prophet Micah:

> Will the Lord be pleased with thousands of rams,
>   with ten thousands of rivers of oil?
> He has showed you, O man, what is good;
>   and what does the Lord require of you
> but to do justice, and to love kindness
>   and to walk humbly with your God?

> (Micah 6:7-8)

(4) Turning is always God's initiative. It is he who first turns to men and women. The prophets speak his word and make his presence known, calling the people to turn to God, who has already turned to them. Their commitment to him follows his commitment to them.

Against this Old Testament background we approach conversion in the New Testament. Standing in the line of the Old Testament prophets, John the Baptist issues a call to conversion, *metanoia*, repentance, which is also a call to bring fruits worthy of repentance (Matt. 3:8).

When Jesus starts his ministry his main theme is: "The time is fulfilled and the kingdom of God is at hand; repent, and believe in the gospel" (Mark 1:15). The kingdom of God is his rule of justice, compassion, and integrity revealed in history and now embodied in Christ. Conversion means becoming a

citizen of this kingdom, a citizenship which is shared in justice
and peace. The kingdom of God is not something one possesses
through individual piety; it is the realm of a life of turning to
each other in love as a result of being turned to the King. This is
something which has to keep happening all the time. The words
"repent" and "believe" are in the present tense: there is nothing
static here. The call is a constant one; and it will be so until the
end of history, when we shall be judged by whether or not we
have turned to our fellow humans in their need, for God has
already turned to them and is present beside them (Matt. 25:31-
46).

Similarly, when the people at Pentecost are challenged to
repent, they immediately form a community of sharing (Acts
2:37-45). Conversion is becoming part of the new covenant
people, a sign of the presence of the kingdom and a witness to
the final promise of history. This is reflected in Paul's words to
the Corinthians, when he speaks of Christians "being changed
into Christ's likeness from one degree of glory to another" (2
Cor. 3:18). Christians of the Orthodox tradition call attention
to the present tense of the verb used here (*metamorphoumetha*),
which suggests the continuous character and goal of conversion. Again in Romans 12:1-2 the apostle stresses the ongoing
process of being transformed by the renewing of our mind to
which we are called. The purpose is that we take our place as
members of the community and employ our gifts for the welfare of all people. Conversion leads to a life of including, not
excluding.

The call to conversion also reverberates through the book of
Revelation. Its disclosure of the final outcome of history, when
God will make all things new and create a new city where
people will share a free life in all its rich variety, is prefaced by
an appeal to the seven young and small churches of Asia Minor
to be converted to the way of the Lord. If the empires and
nations of the world are to be called to repentance and conversion, the church must first be so called. Only thus can it be a
witness of the living God and of his demands to the world.

### The need for conversion

Is the call for conversion to God in Christ an essential part of
a living ministry in today's changing world? There can be no

doubt that the answer is yes — and now more than ever. Let me mention briefly some reasons:

(1) The process of secularization makes people increasingly responsible for themselves and therefore for their fellow humans. No longer is it possible to hide behind the idea that we are the playthings of natural forces. The growing mastery of creation renders humanity all the more accountable for itself and creation. The glory of the natural sciences is that they give us the tools to be emancipated from nature. But the social sciences — and the ordinary facts of everyday life — show clearly that in spite of this immense power men and women remain wrapped up in all sorts of phobias and neuroses, in boredom, alienation, and meaninglessness. Indeed, this process of being turned in on oneself seems to increase as people are drawn closer together through science and technology and ever more developed communications media.

How is the desperate human need to be turned away from self and to and for others to be satisfied? The biblical teaching of the living God who has turned to people in creation, in history, and supremely in Christ, the true man who was always turned towards others because he was turned to God, is more relevant today than ever before. We can never be certain that people will in fact turn to Christ in humble faith, but the issues of conversion can be put more intelligibly than ever before. Yet this call cannot be set before the world unless the church is also constantly being challenged by it.

(2) The universal longing for justice and a humane life is precisely a longing for a life of turning to one another — eye to eye and mouth to mouth. This life together is conceived in terms of mutual recognition and respect and sharing the fruits of creation in justice and common welfare. It is a longing for identity and also for community. The biblical concept of turning speaks directly to these longings. People find their true identity before God, *coram Deo*, and that identity is expressed in their freedom to be before others and *for* them.

Moreover, human longings are matched by God's promise, which has been made alive in Christ and will be fully revealed at the end of time. Turning or conversion means moving to a certain future, a breakaway from the vicious circle of a self-enclosed life and history. Changed by Christ, we can work joyfully for change. Personal transformation is directly related to the task of social and political transformation. That urgent teaching of the Old Testament prophets is very relevant today. Again, unless this understanding of ourselves is being made real within the Christian community we cannot effectively call others to this conversion.

(3) Every ministry performèd in the name of Christ is a call to conversion, for it points to the life of turning to God and others in truth, integrity, justice, and love. Every Christian ministry is concerned to make the presence of God in Christ alive to people and therefore to enable them to hear his call to conversion. The time, the place, and the manner of this call will come as we carry out sensitively the ministry of Christ to people of other faiths and of none. Necessity is laid on us, as Paul says (1 Cor. 9:6), but this necessity carries with it the fulfilment of everything which people are truly seeking and which God offers in Christ. All is of God; therefore we call others to conversion in humility and joy and hope, knowing that the call to others is always a call to ourselves to be constantly converted to Christ and therefore to all people in love.

How could Paul issue the call to conversion with such faith and confidence? Can we tap this same certainty today? The age in which Paul wrote was an age of anxiety. In many ways Corinth was a city in which this anxiety was particularly evident. It stood between the western and eastern Mediterranean, between Greek and Roman culture. It had its rich and its poor, its powerful and its weak, its free people and its slaves, its intellectuals and its unlettered, its Jews with their exclusive faith in God and its Gentiles with their pagan mystery cults. Once a proud Greek city-state, it had been swallowed into the Roman Empire as a colony. Everywhere there were divisions and party strife and anxiety about the future. These attitudes were reproduced in the church of Corinth, as the two New Testament letters of Paul to Corinth make clear.

Our age has also been called an age of anxiety. The divisions in human society today match closely the situation in Corinth. Paul's affirmations to the Corinthians about how to live in the context of anxieties on the strength of the reconciliation which God brings in Christ through his death and resurrection, which we are called both to participate in and to commend to others, thus speak to us.

Two realities confront us: the action and offer of God in Christ and the concrete manifestations of anxiety which are our human lot. Paul does not gloss over this anxiety, which he himself feels acutely. He talks of "afflictions, hardships, beatings, imprisonments, tumults, labours, sleeplessness, hunger, dishonour, ill-repute, being treated as impostors, unknown, dying, punished, miserable, poor, having nothing" (2 Cor. 6:4-5, 8-10). Being human means having anxiety — the anxiety that we are finite and must die, that our lives make no sense, that we have failed to live up to what is demanded of us as responsible persons.

But Christ came to break through the straitjacket of death by taking death on himself and bringing us the endless life of the resurrection. Christ shed the light of meaning on our human existence by his constant communion with God, the source of meaning, and by his untiring self-giving for people in all situations. It was Christ, as Paul boldly says, whom God made "to be sin who knew no sin, so that in him we might become the righteousness of God" (2 Cor. 5:21). By taking on himself our unacceptability to God, he has enabled us to become truly accepted, truly ourselves.

The Reformers recovered this reality in the age of anxiety at the end of the Middle Ages and the opening of the Renaissance. Reading Luther, John Wesley learned this reality at the beginning of the age of anxiety brought about by the Industrial Revolution. It was this reality which my African forefathers discovered when they heard the gospel in the midst of slavery and turned their faith into songs of joy and hope in the Negro spirituals and calypsoes. This reality is offered to us today.

But, as we have been stressing, our turning to the reality of this life in Christ demands that we become collaborators with him in his ministry of reconciliation. We are not to be passive bearers of our own and others' anxieties. Rather we take them actively on ourselves in order to be instruments of God's assault on anxiety. Paul mentions three qualities which those who are converted have to display in living with and conquering anxiety.

(1) The power of God generates within us new possibilities of living with and through anxiety. This is the power of genuine love, which enables us to be open, caring, and patient with others, relentless in disclosing the realities of our existence, and ready to be led by the surprises of the Holy Spirit.

(2) We take on ourselves God's warfare to establish his justice. That means attacking evil and defending against it with what Paul calls "the weapons of justice" (2 Cor. 6:7). The people of God, the church, is called upon to expose the sources of anxiety and to join in the struggle against them. Everything that tends to threaten the dignity and integrity of human beings, to restrict and cramp their humanity, must be tackled in the name of God with the weapons of God.

(3) Such an open existence as servants turned to God and to others is bound to lead us into an ambiguous life. We share in all the anxieties which threaten life in God, and there is no way out of this involvement. "We are treated as impostors and yet true; as unknown and yet well known; as dying, and behold we live; as punished, and yet not killed; as sorrowful, yet always rejoicing; as poor, yet making many rich; as having nothing and yet possessing everything" (2 Cor. 6:8-10).

There is no doubt where Paul stands. He calls us to turn: to surrender our concern for self-affirmation, to live and work for the freedom of others and not our own security, to struggle for the empowerment of the weak and the oppressed, to be unafraid for the sake of the justice, salvation, and liberation which God brings.

## Set free for freedom

The paradox of turning to God and others and turning away from ourselves is that it is precisely this conversion which brings true freedom, genuine liberation.

Mention liberation in our world today and a host of images arises. There are political liberation movements aplenty, seeking through various means to free people from oppressive governments. Millions are struggling for freedom from economic bondage, whether imposed by the power of multinational corporations or unequal distribution of resources and wealthy elites. Racial liberation movements in places like southern Africa strive for human dignity and freedom against the background of centuries of patient endurance which brought no change. The women's liberation movement fights against the entrenched and often blatant discrimination of men against women in society and in the church. Overall, one can detect in all humankind a deep longing for freedom from a wide range of impersonal oppressive structures — in society, in government, in education, and even in the church.

How does turning to God in Christ relate to these desires for liberation? The apostle Paul connects these two themes in Galatians 5; indeed, his entire letter to the Christians of the Roman province of Galatia has been called the great manifesto of Christian liberty.

When Paul and Barnabas first brought the gospel to the Galatian churches, they had run into stiff opposition from Jewish leaders because they claimed that people were saved by faith in Christ alone, not by obedience to the Jewish law. Many pagan Galatians had heard that message gladly and accepted the faith.

Temperamentally, the Galatians were curious, eager to learn, an excited and excitable people. Julius Caesar described them as impelled by the desire for change, with an excessive devotion to external observances. Their restless character was seen by others as instability and self-indulgence. Against this background we can appreciate the boldness of Paul's proclamation that faith in Christ alone makes people free to be themselves and free for others without external props of any kind, whether pagan or Jewish.

But as soon as Paul and Barnabas left this very young Christian community, a group of Jewish Christians began to insist that one could be a Christian only by being circumcised, in other words becoming in effect a Jew. They tried to discredit Paul and his credentials as an apostle and missionary. Confronted by this confusion, the Galatian Christians were in grave danger of giving in: some were inclined to follow Jewish legalism, while the majority would perhaps simply lapse into the pagan ways from which they were just in the process of being liberated (Gal. 4:3, 8-11; 5:15, 19-21).

Paul had discovered true freedom in Christ at great cost to himself. "I have been crucified with Christ," he writes. "It is no longer I that live but Christ who lives in me, and the life I now live in the flesh, I live by faith in the Son of God who loved me and gave himself for me" (Gal. 2:20). Paul had a tremendous sense of God in his freedom coming in Christ, who took on our human nature for what it was and showed us self-giving love totally to the point of the cross, and then came through victoriously in the resurrection. Therefore, those baptized in the death and resurrection of Christ emerge as free human beings, authentically themselves. That is the good news of the Christian faith. Christ sets us free from ourselves, from enslaving cultures and practices which divide and destroy, and makes us free to be ourselves and therefore for others.

But this is no easy matter. Our freedom has to be affirmed all the time. Paul uses the strong phrase "Stand fast" (Gal. 5:1) — which translates a Greek word commonly used in athletics to suggest that in the long race you have to keep going until you reach the end. The forces that seek to imprison us are very strong and subtle. The Jewish thinker Martin Buber commented that "to become free of a bond is destiny." If life lived in freedom is not a personal responsibility it is a pathetic farce. Freedom is a vocation, a call to which we have to respond daily with ourselves. Perhaps the word "liberation" brings out this connotation more clearly than "freedom," which sometimes has a static, inner-related sense rather than the sense of a process.

Christ came to initiate in us this process of liberation from the enslaving elements of our culture, a liberation which can make that culture something living and authentic. That is of course one of the great issues that Christians face today. He or she who hears the voice of Christ can only answer with the voice of his or her own culture, not somebody else's. Christians from many different backgrounds must seek genuine ways to express the universal Christian faith in their own cultures, and these diverse expressions must be respected and encouraged by Christians from other cultures. The freedom to be different, and yet in that difference to be part of the universality of Christ's work, is one element of the freedom which Christ has brought us. The other element is the freedom of the unity (*not* uniformity) of his people.

The unity of the Galatian church was definitely in danger. Had the Jewish Christians succeeded in enforcing circumcision, Christianity would have ended up as a sect and probably disappeared. What Paul was fighting for was the true unity of the church: on the one basis of Christ's death and resurrection for us, and on the one condition of our faith in him, we have a unity in which there is neither Jew nor Gentile, bond nor free, male nor female, but all are one in Christ Jesus (Gal. 3:28). Freedom in Christ is the one condition for the true unity of God's people in this diversity.

But then comes the question of what this freedom or liberation is for. We have noted that liberation is the only way in Christ to become truly oneself and therefore the only way to true unity in diversity. But something deeper is at stake, because one is oneself only in relation to others. What is the true relation to others? Paul says we are free to love. That is the only worthwhile freedom, based on the Christ who loved me and gave himself for me. When Charles Wesley read Luther's comment about this passage on Pentecost Sunday in 1738, it struck him as such an explosively new thing that it made him, so to speak, jump out of his illness into being the greater singer of Methodism — six to seven thousand hymns. He had found this Saviour of mankind, who had taught him how to love the whole world.

The condition of true freedom is a faith which works itself out in love (Gal. 5:6). We cannot have this love by ourselves; it is God's Spirit in us who frees us in spontaneous expression of this love. The fruit of the Spirit is love. All the other things Paul lists in verses 22 and 23 are only expressions of this one great fruit of love. How does it operate? First of all in recognizing "who is my neighbour."

Paul phrases the call to love our neighbour in terms of bearing each other's burdens (Gal. 6:2). Interestingly enough, three verses later he says that everyone "will have to bear his own load." The two words here have different senses: a "burden" is that which one cannot carry by himself or herself; but bearing one's own load speaks of that which is proper to one — one's physical and intellectual and spiritual endowments, that which one is free to be. It is only when we freely carry out what we are that we are free to bear the heavy load of others.

In his freedom Paul could say, "I bear on my body the marks of Jesus" (Gal. 6:17). Bearing the cross is the freest act we can do, because it was on the cross that God's freedom was mani-

fest for us. And while we live in an unfree world, we are called
to bear the cross so that others may be free. A Christian in the
world today is thus one who, having received freedom, has
been called to freedom — not the freedom of self-indulgence,
but freedom in Christ, which we express by being ourselves and
being for others in love.

*The promise of life in all its fullness*

To exercise the freedom to live for others, this freedom which
Paul sees as a calling as well as a gift, is to live life in its fullness. Such abundant life was the promise of Jesus, as recorded
in his last public discourse: "I have come that men may have
life, and may have it in all its fullness" (John 10:10).

But what does this marvelous phrase mean for us? How do
we make it real for ourselves? What obstacles stand in the way
of attaining it? And how can we share life in its fullness with
others for whom life is often an empty prelude to death?

In John 10:7-18 Jesus outlines three elements to this fullness
of life.

First of all, life in all its fullness means safety — the freedom
(to use Jesus' imagery of sheep) to go in and out and find good
pasture (v. 9). In this torn and divided world all sorts of barriers
have been built and maintained to prevent free movement and
exchange between peoples and cultures. The resources of the
earth, which should be for the benefit of all, are hoarded by the
few. God's purpose is for his creation to be like a vast pasturage
which provides sustenance and life for all.

Life in its fullness also means knowing one another, sharing
in a common life together, being mutually aware of and caring
for one another. "I know my own sheep, and my sheep know
me — as the Father knows me and I know the Father" (vv.
14-15). In our torn world, knowledge is often sought because it
can bring the power to exploit the creation and other human
beings. In the purpose of God, knowledge means being related
to one another and being for one another. Research and technology, economic and social and political science should have
no purpose other than to enable human beings to understand
each other more fully and to use creation for good. That was
God's intention when he created human beings, male and
female, as custodians of creation.

Finally, life in its fullness means fullness for all. God's purpose is that all should share a common life in one fold (v. 16). Our torn world provides a sort of fullness of life for a few, and penury and death for the many. In fact those who enjoy the good things of life at the expense of the rest of humankind lead a mean and narrow existence. They are like those who sought to build the Tower of Babel to reach up to the heavens and to make a name for themselves, as successive civilizations and empires have done, and transnational enterprises today, only to come crashing down in confusion and conflict.

The story of the Tower of Babel (Gen. 11:1-6) brings to a climax the first chapters of Genesis, which describe the creation of all things, especially humanity, and report how human beings time and again revolted against the purpose of God and fought with each other. Adam and Eve could neither respond to God nor be responsible to one another because they rebelled against God and sought to conform to creation in the form of the serpent rather than to the way of God. Cain felt no responsibility for his brother Abel — "Am I my brother's keeper?" — and so felt free to kill him. From there it is only a few short steps to this monolithic effort to set up a human structure of power and prestige that would reach from earth to heaven. The Tower of Babel is, indeed, the symbol of all our human efforts.

But the Bible goes on to tell another story in Genesis 12. God calls one man, Abraham, out of his city, Ur of the Chaldees, to make a new start. To him is the promise that all the families of the earth will be blessed. The sense of "bless" in Hebrew is to share one's life and power with another, to be with him or her — and that means sharing the life and power of God, which manifests itself in justice, love, and peace. That is why the vision at the end of the Bible, in Revelation 21-22, is of the new city of Jerusalem, through whose gates, which are open to all, the nations bring their full riches to be shared by all. Even the leaves of the tree of life will no longer be used to make profit, but will be available for the healing of the nations.

This is what Jesus is saying when he offers fullness of life for all who form one flock under one shepherd. And Christ's offer of fullness for all is at the same time a challenge to Christian obedience. Just as conversion means turning to God and others, just as freedom means turning away from self-indulgence to bearing others' burdens, so fullness of life means a commitment to offer that fullness to everyone. It is this understanding, for example, which undergirds all Christian efforts to work for a more just economic order.

Such efforts have nothing to do with the materialistic and unbiblical idea that abundance of possessions ensures happiness. But those who have heard the call of Jesus will recognize that economic systems and orders are the creation of human beings. Consequently, it is persons who are the bearers of life or of death. No order or system or enterprise can function without the human beings who create and operate it. We who are made in the image of God are called to be co-workers with him in manifesting and sharing life in all its fullness. Newness must start with us.

That is what the gospel asserts. Created in God's likeness, we must be re-created in the image of his Son Jesus Christ. In John 10 Jesus presents himself as the Good Shepherd. Both parts of this phrase are important. The shepherd is an ancient biblical image for the ruler whose task it was to care for the sheep in justice. The classic passage in the Bible about this is Ezekiel 34:1-5, where God says:

> You shepherds, these are the words of the Lord God: How I hate the shepherds of Israel who care only for themselves! Should not the shepherd care for the sheep? You consume the milk, wear the wool, and slaughter the fat beasts, but you do not feed the sheep. You have not encouraged the weary, tended the sick, bandaged the hurt, recovered the straggler, or searched for the lost; and even the strong you have driven with ruthless severity. They are scattered, they have no shepherd, they have become the prey of wild beasts.

But the prophet adds:

> For these are the words of the Lord God: Now I myself will ask after my sheep and go in search of them.... I will feed them on good grazing-ground.... I myself will tend my flock, I myself pen them in their fold, says the Lord God. I will search for the lost, recover the straggler, bandage the hurt, strengthen the sick, leave the healthy and strong to play, and give them their proper food (vv. 11-16).

Jesus is the Shepherd *par excellence*. And he is called "good" (*kalos*), a word which means attractive rather than repellent, noble, honourable, of fine quality, excellent, thorough, efficient, dependable, not just good in itself but *seen* to be good. *Kalos* is the word used in the Greek version of Genesis 1 for God's assessment of creation: "God saw all that he had made and it was very good" — that is, what he intended and what he did were one, the expression of his self-giving love for all.

Several characteristics of the Good Shepherd emerge from John 10. He makes life safe and free for the sheep to find pasturage (v. 9), even at the risk of his own life (vv. 11, 15). He knows the sheep and they know him. Between them there is an open intimacy which makes for coherence between thought and act in sacrificial service (v. 15). Working for fullness of life for all (v. 16), the Good Shepherd sees his task as a freely accepted mandate given by the source of being, the Father, our Creator God (v. 18).

By contrast, there are also those who set up obstacles to life in all its fullness. They are the thieves (who steal by guile) and the robbers (who steal openly by force). These set out not only to steal but to kill and destroy (vv. 8, 10). These are the exploiters, the manipulators of the economy, the ravagers of the earth's resources, the cynical arms merchants, the bullying imperialists, the militaristic régimes, the torturers, the violators of human rights. They work their destruction all over the world, and no nation is exempt from its effects. But there are also the hirelings, the paid functionaries. Concerned only about their own interests and profit, they are quick to run from any responsibility when danger comes (vv. 12-13). Such lack of responsibility is also widespread in today's world. It is typical of the faceless agents of giant military-industrial complexes, who feel responsible to no one except their often equally faceless employers. Devoid of deep human convictions, they care for no one except themselves and their immediate relations and friends.

The choice before us is clear: Shall we be good shepherds or thieves and robbers and hirelings? It is a harsh choice, but an inescapable one laid on us by God through his word and in the cries of suffering and exploited humanity.

What is to be done? Vladimir Lenin once asked that question. But he discounted religious faith altogether. He was an ideological Marxist atheist, and the system he helped to set up has become faceless and ruthless — one more tragic occasion for asking "what is to be done?" But there are plenty of practical atheists around as well, people who believe that all that is needed is to think up and set in motion orders, systems, enterprises, and let the principle of the survival of the fittest do its work. The results of this human self-sufficiency are all around in this torn world. Only as we commit ourselves to Jesus Christ, the Good Shepherd, shall we receive life in all its fullness and share it with others.

# 3. The call to be advocates

We have seen that the biblical understandings of salvation, conversion, freedom, and life in its fullness all point beyond the promise of blessing for the individual to a wider perspective. To work out our salvation means rejecting self-centredness in a spirit of self-giving for others. To be converted is to turn, not only to God, but to our fellow human beings. True freedom in Christ has to be affirmed in a faith that works itself out in love. Life in all its fullness is a promise which at the same time calls us to obedience and sharing.

This presents a decisive challenge to the world and its values. The Romans had a saying that realistically and starkly captured those values: "Man is a wolf to man." This chilling truth is the logical outcome of self-centredness, self-indulgence, and the struggle for self-sufficiency. What Christ revealed and taught was the self-emptying love of God; and in John 15, calling himself the vine, he exhorts those who would follow him to bear fruit. Note well the imagery here: the disciples are called to *bear* fruit, not to gather it. Getting and grabbing — rather than offering and giving — is the way of the world.

Jesus gives the disciples the commandment "that you love one another as I have loved you. Greater love has no man than this, that a man lay down his life for his friends" (vv. 12-13). The world loves those who share the mistrust, greed, competitive attitudes, and ideological antagonisms which are the result of sin. We see that time and again in the relations between nations, races, tribes, castes, classes, and individuals.

It is in such a world that the Christian church exists. Too often in history it has reflected that world in its own life and in

its support of those who are in power. Today the church everywhere is a minority. No longer does it exercise power and
authority in society, no longer is it loved by the world. Blaise
Pascal wrote about the church in seventeenth-century France:
"The condition of the church is good when it has or seeks no
other support than that given by its Lord." This is what the
Confessing Church learned in Germany during the struggle
against Fascism. That is what all our churches have to learn
today.

### The coming of the Paraclete

So how can the church live in a hostile world today? What
are the resources given to us, and what is our task? Jesus assures
us of the coming of the Paraclete — the Counselor, the Com-
forter — the Spirit of Truth who comes from the Father and
witnesses to Christ. This word from the Lord was a great conso-
lation to the church of the first generation, and we today must
attend to it no less carefully.

The Spirit, the life-giving power of God, is described in three
ways which are relevant for us as we face our situation: as the
Paraclete, as the one who communicates the truth, and as the
one who witnesses to Christ (John 15:26 - 16:4).

*Parakletos* in Greek means one who is called beside another,
one who comes to the aid of others, who acts as an advocate,
opening out the issues which are at stake. The gospel says that
the Paraclete is sent from beside the Father to be beside us. He
is therefore the living, revealing, exposing, caring presence of
God the Father, in the same way as Jesus was — among his disciples and to the people. His being beside us is explained further as communicating the truth. Truth in Jesus' language sig-
naled God's faithfulness and trustworthiness. Much more than
an idea, it is a personal word, with connotations of trust and
openness, of being what one is and is called to be. Truth in
Greek means literally the state of being uncovered, being disclosed, opened out. What is true is what shows itself in all its
depth. It is not hidden or disguised, not wrapped up in itself,
not confused by lies and propaganda.

In fact, truth has been revealed in Christ. "I am the truth," he
says (John 14:6). The task of the Spirit is to witness to the incarnate truth in Jesus — to disclose, expose, open out the meaning

of all that Christ was and did for us. That is what Jesus promised his disciples: receiving the Spirit at Pentecost they were given a totally new direction, a new power and boldness, a new creativity and community — and we today are the heirs of all that.

This is why it is essential for us to hear the words of Christ: "You also are witnesses" (15:27). The gift of the Spirit, this life-giving power of God which opens up the whole of reality, is not like a possession for us. It is not intended to give us some safe and superior haven from a wicked world. Christ's promise and gift are for us to continue his witness to God's faithfulness and trustworthiness, to reality in the world as it is and for the sake of what it might become in Christ. What does this mean for us today?

First, we too are called to be Paracletes, to comfort and counsel one another. We are called to be beside each other, helping, exhorting, consoling, strengthening. That is what fellowship within our congregations and churches and between the churches around the world is all about. Even when Jesus' disciples failed him, he did not leave them, but gave himself up for them, and appeared to them with his peace, breathing his Spirit upon them. Our fellowship in the Spirit with Christ therefore enables us to be beside others, in solidarity with them as brothers and sisters for whom Christ died, whether they accept him or not.

That is what the churches today are trying to do within the ecumenical movement. Through programmes of inter-church aid we go wherever there is need to be beside those who suffer and are deprived. Through the World Council of Churches' Programme to Combat Racism, through its Commission on the Churches' Participation in Development, and through the renewal groups with which the WCC is in touch, we show our solidarity with the oppressed and seek to make them aware of their condition in a new way and to participate in their own liberation in justice and community.

Such corporate efforts parallel what courageous persons have done through the ages and in our time. To name only one example, Martin Luther King was a person who allowed himself to be grasped and sent forth by the Spirit with the vision of a reconciled humanity. With the word of the Spirit he went

beside his fellow black people who were oppressed and also
beside the white people who were oppressors, dreaming the
dream of a united society. He did this fully conscious of the
risks he was taking, yet with the love and joy and peace and
boldness of one seized by the Spirit. He was assassinated, but
his witness remains — a witness not to himself but to the one
who was crucified and rose again. It is a witness of God's
future, his establishment of the reality of our lives according to
his design.

In the second place, we are called as those who are filled with
the Spirit to witness to the truth. "He who does what is true
comes to the light," John's gospel says, "*that it may be clearly
seen that his deeds have been wrought by God*" (3:21). And
Jesus' prayer for his disciples is that God will "sanctify them in
the truth" (John 17:17). We are committed to be real persons in
our attitudes, words, and actions, and to uncover the reality of
our situations according to God's word revealed in Christ.

This is not something that can be done once and for all.
Every period in history calls for a disclosure of its own inner
depth, its own possibilities for good and evil. Christians are in a
particularly advantageous position for doing this with the word
of God in the Bible and the experience of the church during
nearly two thousand years. But this privilege brings with it a terrible responsibility, which we neglect at our peril, no matter
what the inducements to avoid our responsibility. The world
today is paradoxical in this regard: the revolution in communications and the development of psychology have made available many sophisticated new ways of uncovering and exposing
things and people, but this can be done in a most cynical way,
whose object is not to reveal or disclose but to disguise and
destroy. These means are employed to cover up reality and
build up a world of make-believe, of transient values, of propaganda, of exploiting people's unconscious drives and wishes.

The truth of which Jesus speaks, on the other hand, enables
people to become their true selves. It discloses God's world in a
way which is for the welfare of all, which builds up rather than
destroys. As Paul put it, we must speak and do the truth in love,
being beside others in good will and caring.

When Jesus prays that his disciples may be sanctified in the
truth, that is, that they may themselves become wholly com-

mitted to being genuine and making things and people genuine, he also prays that they may be *one*, so that the world may believe. This is the reality behind the ecumenical movement. As we learn to be open with and listen to each other, as we seek the prophetic vision to see into the heart of things in the perspective of God's justice and faithfulness, as we commit ourselves to one another in fellowship, we shall be better vehicles of truth, of reality, of God's purpose for mankind. That is the aim of all the studies and programmes undertaken by the World Council of Churches, whether they concern faith and order, mission, dialogue with people of living faiths and ideologies, church and society, education, human rights, or any other area. We are opening ourselves to receive from each other that truth which alone can lead to the unity of God's people and the unity of humankind.

Christ's promise and gift are sure — the Spirit of truth, the Paraclete who witnesses to him and enables us to witness. But how do we appropriate this promise and gift? The world is strong, indeed overpowering. Moreover, its untruth, divisiveness, and brutality are within us as well, and in our churches. We are sorely tempted to give up, to fall away because the task is too great for us. Not long after the disciples heard these words of Jesus, they forsook him and fled at the time of his trial. After his burial, they hid behind closed doors. But the risen Lord broke through those closed doors with his word of peace and with his offer: "Receive the Holy Spirit" (John 20:22). He sent them forth into the world with the reminder "In the world you have tribulation; but be of good cheer, I have overcome the world." He sends us forth in the power of this same Holy Spirit.

## The Spirit and the call to unity

Overcoming the divisions of the Christian church which have arisen since the dramatic fulfilment on Pentecost of Jesus' promise to send the Paraclete has been a major preoccupation of the ecumenical movement. The link between the gift of the Holy Spirit and Christ's prayer for unity has been a prominent ecumenical theme. When four hundred delegates of the churches met at the First World Conference on Faith and Order in Lausanne in 1927, they issued a stirring "Call to Unity":

God's Spirit has been in the midst of us. It was he who called us hither. His presence has been manifest in our worship, our delibera-tions and our whole fellowship. He has discovered us to one another. He has enlarged our horizons, quickened our under-standing, and enlivened our hope. We have dared and God has jus-tified our daring.

Indeed, the churches and Christians have never been the same again. Since then groups have gathered in prayer and study for the unity of the church. The Week of Prayer for Chris-tian Unity, proposed in 1918, has become a yearly reality for all our churches. Out of their isolation churches have drawn together more closely — timidly at first, more naturally with the years. Today nearly all the churches of the world are in fellow-ship with each other, rather than in ignorance, rivalry, and even enmity. Since 1948 the Orthodox, Anglican, and other churches of the Reformation and of the later evangelical awakening have joined together in the World Council of Churches. Today there are nearly 300 of these churches in over 100 countries around the world.

During these fifty years, churches have grown together in mutual understanding. Councils of churches have been formed in most countries and continents. And since the Second Vatican Council, the Roman Catholic Church has opened itself to other churches. The *Traduction Oecuménique de la Bible*, completed in 1975 by Roman Catholic, Orthodox, and Protestant scholars, was a great achievement. What is astonishing about this transla-tion are the agreed brief exegetical notes on the text, facilitating corporate and private Bible study. An ecumenical hymnbook, *Cantate Domino*, contains the musical treasures, old and new, of all our churches. Youth, students, lay people, women, priests and pastors — together and in their different groupings — meet regularly to affirm and grow in their faith and to seek ways of witnessing together in today's world. Two such groups which have been very active are the Taizé community and the Foco-lare movement.

The delegates at Lausanne in 1927 recognized that profound historical and doctrinal issues separated the churches. Since then there has been a steady flow of ecumenical statements marking new understandings and agreements, and old controversial issues have been reformulated in a way that can draw churches closer together.

We might easily extend the list of ecumenical achievements. Indeed, one might become triumphalistic about what has been done in the last fifty years, especially when it is seen against the background of centuries of division, competition, and sinful disobedience to the will of God. But the fact is that too much has been left undone. Too much remains to be done.

Our first task is to overcome inertia, fatigue, and loss of the nerve to devote ourselves to the unity of the church. Bishop Charles Brent, a great American pioneer of the movement for unity, said in 1910: "Unity, visible and invisible, is not an accident of the gospel; it *is* the gospel." We are not faithful to the gospel if we are not eager to work for the unity of God's people as a sign of the unity of the Godhead. Brent quoted from Paul's letter to the Ephesians in his sermon in Lausanne in 1927: "There is one body and one Spirit, just as you were called to the one hope that belongs to your call, one Lord, one faith, one baptism, one God and Father of us all, who is above all and through all and in all" (4:4-6).

This short confession of faith is the expression of a fact: "There is one Spirit, one Lord, one God and Father of us all, one faith, one baptism, one body." That is the givenness of our lives. It is not something we create ourselves, but the gift of the triune God. As Paul asked the factious Corinthian Christians: "What have you that you did not receive? If then you received it, why do you boast as if it were not a gift?" (1 Cor. 4:7). God's gifts are to be shared. What we are we must become; and we can only become what we are when, like the blessed Trinity, we are ready to include all who call on the name of the God and Father of our Lord Jesus Christ. There is an inescapable demand upon us here. Faithfulness to the gospel means expressing its unity in word and in deed in the fellowship of those who bear the name of him who is the gospel. To be indifferent to the unity of the church as the body of Christ is to be indifferent to Christ.

But who is this Christ in whose name we were baptized and whose name we bear? According to Ephesians, he is the head of the church, "the fullness of him who fills all in all" (1:23). But it is he who in his life, death, resurrection, and ascension has filled all things with the life of God (4:8-10). In fact God's design is "to unite all things in him, things in heaven and things on earth" (1:10). And we are all called to attain to the fullness of our beings as men and women, "to the measure of the stature of the fullness of Christ" (4:13).

What all this means is that to be in Christ, to confess this one Lord, is to participate in his work of uniting all peoples and all things into him. The unity of the church which is his body is the sign and sacrament of the unity of humanity into the fullness of the stature of Christ. The unity of the church is thus not an ecclesiastically domestic affair. It concerns the whole human race. Just as the divisions and conflicts of the churches are signs and reflections of the divisions in our world, so the unity of the church is a sign and sacrament of God's purpose to unite all into Christ as the head of a new humanity and a new creation.

What then is to be done? We are called to overcome barriers between human beings — barriers of race, sex, wealth and poverty, political conflict. Our world is becoming a global village, and the closer we come together the greater the conflicts. Our churches find themselves in the midst of these conflicts. They are part of them and they have contributed to them. The call to the unity of the church is therefore a challenge to resolve the conflicts. Our one baptism means, as Paul says to the Galatians, that "as many of you as were baptized in Christ have put on Christ. There is neither Jew nor Gentile, slave nor free, there is neither male nor female; for you are all one in Christ Jesus" (3:27-28). Racial, cultural, class, and sex divisions have bedeviled the church and the world through the centuries. The struggle for racial and social justice and for the community of women and men in church and society is directly related to the struggle for the one church renewed in the image of God, the fullness of the Christ who fills all in all. Indeed, we are discovering that as Christians enter into this struggle of breaking down barriers in the world they are discovering their unity in Christ.

Paul tells us to be "eager to maintain the unity of the Spirit in the bond of peace" (Eph. 4:3). But it is Christ who is our peace, who through his blood on the cross broke down the walls of hostility between peoples and persons that he might create a new humanity (Eph. 2:14-16). The call to the unity of the church, the body of Christ, is the call to bear the cross of being the instrument of God's peace in the world. Churches and Christians who are engaged in the cause of promoting peace are being drawn together into a new and deeper unity.

Bishop Brent showed in his own life the integral character of the search for the unity of the church. Of his experience in the Philippines he said: "It was among the pagan people that I learned the equality before God of all men which I count to be the chief treasure I have honestly made my own in my life-time." Soon he was led into the struggle against the evil effects of opium, and in 1909 he presided over an international conference on the subject in Shanghai. A year later he began to speak strongly about the urgent necessity of the unity of the church. After World War I he expressed the conviction that "unity of heart and hands among the Churches is the sole hope for the Great Peace." For Brent, the recognition of a common humanity with people of other races and cultures, the struggle against social evils like the opium traffic, the commitment to the cause of world peace, and the striving for the unity of the church were all one call of obedience to Christ.

### The spirituality of unity

How does our work for the unity of the church differ from the efforts of those many other persons and groups working for peace and justice, health and community, and the unity of humanity in the world today? Paul tells us that "grace was given to each of us according to the measure of Christ's gift" (Eph. 4:7). Grace, God's self-giving love, his commitment to us and to all human beings in Christ, is what makes us what we are and enables us to work for the unity of the church. But this grace is varied: "His gifts were that some should be apostles, some prophets, some evangelists, some pastors and teachers, for the equipment of the saints for the work of the ministry, for building up the Body of Christ until we all attain to the unity of the faith and of the knowledge of the Son of God, to complete adulthood, to the measure of the stature of the fullness of Christ" (Eph. 4:11-13). The saints, the people who are committed to God and to his purpose, must be equipped for their ministry, their service, for building up the Body of Christ into the unity of faith. And this is done with the aid of those who preach and teach the word and witness to the one faith.

I believe that the cause of unity will be advanced only as we share more intensely in a common study of the word of God and of the rich traditions of understanding that word through the centuries. I believe that such mutual study in prayer and worship should lead to and be inspired by our common witness to Christ and his work of reconciliation and healing for every human being. That is the experience of churches and Christians in many parts of the world today. I would mention in particular Latin America, where an intensive renewal of the churches has been taking place through Bible study, theological reflection, and prayer in the midst of the struggle for a just society against oppressive forces. Roman Catholics and Protestants, long divided and hostile, are now finding each other in the word and in common witness. In this way they are discovering their work of service in society to overcome the alienation which comes from the class divisions, especially between rich and poor. Only such a passion for the centre of our faith and its proclamation in word and deed can make us "unitable."

The ecumenical movement was conceived in prayer. It was our Lord's own prayer "that they may all be one" (John 17:21) which gave the impetus to Christians to challenge and break down centuries-old barriers. Participation in the ecumenical movement today therefore requires us to say with the disciples: "Lord, teach us to pray." The primary expression of our unity and the first sign of our fellowship as churches and as Christians is the recognition that we all belong to one Father and that we can approach him only through one Lord Jesus Christ.

Our Lord's response to this request was the one prayer which unites us all across our confessions, cultures, and controversies. Here the *how* and the *what* of prayer are brought together. Our attitudes, words, and actions are integral to our total relation to God and to one another. The Lord's Prayer goes to the heart of the ecumenical movement. Its simplicity, straightforwardness, and brevity express the attitude we ought to have to God and to one another. All our massive theological and liturgical structures, our attempts to impress each other by eloquence or persuasiveness, are of no value in opening the way to true dialogue with God or each other. We must discover how to speak and

act simply and directly with each other. This we do only by following our Lord's example in prayer.

Our unity as Christians is constantly affirmed in the way we
address God: "Our Father." No one who truly says "Our
Father" can ever again patronize another person or allow himself or herself to be patronized. Instead, we recognize every
other person, whether near or far, as our sister or brother. Our
prayer is therefore never only for ourselves or "our people," but
is also with and for all. Prayer is always including, never
excluding.

Unity can only be real as we acknowledge our commitment
to God in his inner being and power, and to his kingly rule
present and future — your kingdom come! What draws us
together is not a desire to create some world civilization or a
Christendom based on human power and wisdom (history has
already judged us in this regard), but to put ourselves on the
way of God's purpose. The unity we struggle for is made
human and concrete by the prayer for bread for today and tomorrow. The Psalmist says: "The earth is the Lord's and the fullness thereof; the world (*oikoumene*) and they that dwell
therein" (Psalm 24:1). Our prayer for bread is a recognition
that all we have and create belongs to God and is therefore to
be shared. The ecumenical movement, which forces us to
become painfully conscious of the Christian calling to work for
a just society, is justified in this simple prayer. As God is *our*
Father, that is, the Father of all people, so *our* daily bread is for
all people — not in some distant future but today.

There can be no unity without constant awareness of our
limitations, our failures, our selfish attitudes and acts as individuals, societies, and churches. The prayer for forgiveness is the
indisputable road to unity, because it places on us the inescapable responsibility to forgive one another, individually and corporately. Our fundamental mistrust for one another can only be
overcome by a recognition of our unity in the need for forgiveness. Nor can our common search for unity be maintained
unless we are realistic about the obstacles both in ourselves as
persons and churches and in the world around us. Only our
Father can enable us to have the wisdom and strength to be
loyal to him and to each other in the midst of all that seems to
frustrate his purpose.

The unity of the church is also unity around the sacraments. We have made great progress in accepting each other as sharing one baptism. But what of the one eucharist? There has been considerable agreement about the meaning and the centrality of the eucharist, but there is equally great hesitation about sharing the one eucharist. This has been and is a burning issue among us. Intercommunion is not a battle-cry of Protestant malcontents shrilly outcried by well-armed Catholic stalwarts. It is the deepest inner reality of the people of God, without which they cannot truly render a common witness to the world.

When people who have received the one baptism and have been incorporated into the Body of Christ submit themselves together to the one word of God in the context of one world, rejoice in common praise, repent together in common prayer, hear together God's call to willing and obedient service, they gain a deep and abiding sense of the presence of the Holy Spirit binding them together into a true community of the people of God called to live in and for the world. Is there not a new and wonderful unity given here which demands that it be sealed with receiving the one bread and the one cup of the body and blood of Christ? Is there not in such an ecumenical fellowship something manifestly given which shatters confessional barriers and our ecumenical rules concerning intercommunion? Are the people of God, mobilized for carrying on God's warfare in the world, to be denied together the rations he offers in the body and blood of his Son? Are we not devaluating the depth and reality of holy communion, especially as those who are thus caught into a new manifest unity feel more profoundly the sense of being members incorporate in the Body of Christ than they do in their local denominational communities?

But whatever decisions we make on this matter we must never forget Paul's exhortation to us about our attitude to one another: "with all humility and meekness, with patience, forbearing one another in love" (Eph. 4:2).

The preceding pages have indicated a few of the tasks before us as Christians seeking the unity of the church. But we conclude where we began: the unity we seek has its source in the Holy Spirit. It was on Pentecost that the people gathered together responded to the preaching of Peter by asking: "Brethren, what shall we do?" Peter answered: "Repent, and be baptized, every one of you in the name of Jesus Christ for the forgiveness of your sins; and you shall receive the gift of the Holy Spirit. For the promise is to you and to your children and to all that are far off, every one whom the Lord our God calls to him" (Acts 2:37-39). Those words are no less appropriate today. As people who have been baptized in the name of Jesus Christ, who repent and believe and receive the forgiveness of our sins, we must continue to be open to the gift of the Holy Spirit, so that in unity with Christ we can go forth boldly to live that unity with his people and with all peoples.

# 4. Unity in covenant through the power of love

A helpful outline of how the World Council of Churches is seeking to respond, under the guidance of the Spirit, to the call for unity and to the Lord's mandate that we be *Paracletes*, present with all of humanity, is provided by three programme guidelines formulated at the Fifth Assembly in Nairobi in 1975. These statements speak of the quality of a truly ecumenical fellowship, of the need for authentically incarnating the Christian faith in all historical circumstances, and of the call to participate in the struggle for human dignity and social justice.

## A covenant relationship

A truly ecumenical fellowship is one in which we as churches seek, in communion with Christ and with each other, to relate ourselves, with the fullness of the gospel, to all that is human. The programmes undertaken to achieve this "should become living expressions of the covenant relationship among the churches."

What is the nature of this covenant relationship? Covenant is so central to our faith and life that even the Bible is called the Old and New Covenant ("Testament" being the Latin form of the word). Covenants have always been means by which persons or peoples have entered into relationships on the basis of a community of interests and purpose and in order to maintain those interests and fulfil the purpose. In a divided world, with all its competing interests and powers, this has been necessary in order to maintain any viable existence as nations and peoples.

But in the Bible the covenant is always between God and his people. He is the subject, the one who initiates the covenant relationship and lays down the conditions for it. When God called Abraham out of his particular nation, culture, and religion in Ur of the Chaldees and sent him out to create a new community within another nation, culture, and religion in Canaan, he did a radically new thing in history. In Abraham God broke into our varied cultures and histories to create a community which includes all peoples and cultures under his sovereign will and purpose for the well-being of all.

God says to Abraham: "Behold, my covenant is with you, and you shall be the father of a multitude of nations" (Gen. 17:4). Earlier he told him: "I will bless you, and make your name great, so that you will be a blessing... and by you all the families of the earth will be blessed" (Gen. 12:2-3). The word "bless," *barak*, means to communicate one's strength, one's vitality, one's self to another, to enable another to be vigorous and effective in achieving his or her aims — in brief, to *be with* the other. Thus the covenant is that bond which God creates with and between his people by which they receive his life and power and share it with each other.

When Christ comes as the inaugurator of the new covenant he is named "the son of Abraham" (Matt. 1:1). He fulfils the promise made to Abraham. In him the life and power of God are outpoured in self-giving love for all humankind. "My body given for you... my blood shed for you." That is the heart of the covenant relationship. In ancient Israel one spoke of "cutting a covenant": the covenant was sealed when the people shared the flesh of the sacrificial victim in a community meal. We too are children of Abraham when by faith in Christ we dare to reach out to one another in blessing one another, sharing the life of God in us with each other. But we can only share this life of God as we receive it daily in worship and in his word and do so together and for one another.

As the Abrahamic, pilgrim people of God we are called to make real in our time this covenant fellowship of sharing and offering the life of God to "all the families of the earth." That is the *raison d'être* of the ecumenical movement. This covenant fellowship is not an optional extra to our normal existence as Christians and as churches, but an inescapable obligation upon us. The central task of the ecumenical movement is to make this obligation an ever-increasing reality. Thus the guideline that all the programmes of the World Council of Churches should express and further the covenant relationship of the member churches is rightly given first place.

What are some of the consequences of this guideline?

(1) *An intimate fellowship.* The World Council and its member churches must be clearly seen to be in intimate relationship with each other. No longer can they behave as though they have a sort of separate existence. For too long there has been a kind of *apartheid* in the relations between the churches and the World Council, with only occasional and well-defined times of meeting and of acting, for example, at an assembly or in the appointment of committee members. Too many of our member churches, whose leaders may participate actively in the work of the World Council, do not see their church's involvement in the life and work of the WCC as an indispensable part of its calling.

There is no use throwing around statistics about "three hundred member churches in nearly a hundred countries" unless these churches share in this God-given demand of the interpenetration of their life within the fellowship of the WCC. I consider the establishment of much closer and more intimate relations with member churches as a primary task. There is no future for the ecumenical movement or for the WCC without this inner mutuality between the churches and the Council. And the member churches, no matter how rich and important and self-sufficient they feel, live a truncated and impoverished existence if they are unwilling to share their life with others and receive from them.

(2) *Working more closely together.* It becomes more and more incumbent on the World Council to be so involved in the life of its member churches that its real existence cannot be ignored. We have too often failed to go beyond the more formal kinds of communication with the churches to a real intermingling of programme and effort, in which neither the Council nor the churches can ignore one another. Increasing the budget for our Communication Department does not go to the nerve of the issue. It is a state of mind and attitude we are facing here. We must find imaginative ways for the churches to take part in

shaping and carrying out, together through the Council, tasks essential for their renewal and witness as they seek to become more united to Christ and to one another.

I indicated earlier the meaning of the word "bless" in Hebrew. There is the opposite word, "curse," *qillel* or *'arar* in Hebrew, which means to withdraw one's support from another, to leave alone, to be aloof from or desert the other, so that he or she becomes weak, directionless, and so loses weight, cracks up, becomes lifeless, and is destroyed. The issue before the churches and the Council is as clear as that: will the relationship be one of blessing or of cursing? We cannot be comfortable about the persistent signs of a curse which seem to hang over us. We must labour to lift this curse and place ourselves on the way of the blessing of our common Lord.

(3) *Reaching the congregations.* The relations between the World Council and the member churches can only become a living reality in each place at the local levels of the churches' existence. Of course, in practice it is extremely difficult to see how the Council can operate directly with the congregations, since it is so difficult to have a viable, meaningful relationship with the churches as a whole. Some might even argue that the WCC would be acting unconstitutionally and irresponsibly if it dealt directly with congregations. However, after the Second Assembly in Evanston in 1954, the World Council embarked on a big effort to mobilize the laity, that 99% of the membership of the churches often described as the "frozen assets of the church." A great deal was achieved in the following years in making both the churches and the World Council conscious of this ministry of the laity. The time has come to face the logic of this challenge.

The laity, the *laos*, the people of God, are in fact the congregations and communities where Christian work and worship, witness and spiritual nourishment take place. The concept of conciliar fellowship will remain a slogan if it does not express itself in each place in the ways by which Christians old and young, men and women, of different walks of life and different confessions seek to live in council together for the sake of a more authentic confession of Christ in the world. More specifically, this conciliar fellowship must manifest itself in mutual intercession, with congregations praying for each other, participating in each other's spirituality, pleading the world's needs before God, and receiving his grace to minister to those needs.

There is no doubt that in the coming years the Council will have to give major emphasis to how congregations can be helped to be vital centres for Christian life, mission, and service. I hope we can respond with the same enthusiasm, enterprise, and imagination as in the post-Evanston period when we promoted the ministry of the laity.

(4) *Relations with other bodies*. This covenant relationship among the churches must be seen to be alive in each place and in all places. The WCC cannot be alone in promoting this fellowship. National Christian councils and the regional conferences of churches must play a vital role. There is a close but uneasy relationship between the World Council and the regional and national councils — a relationship which is all the more uneasy because the member churches are so little committed to either the national, regional, or world councils. The problem does not lie in the tasks to be done. A quick survey of the programmes of the various councils indicates that we all have similar concerns and activities. Rather we have to learn how to be sensitive to each other and how to act together and for each other. General consultations have proved to be unfruitful. There will have to be intensive encounter with each of these councils to discover how we can be mutually supportive.

The same can be said about the relations of the World Council with the World Confessional Families. Much is happening between and within the various confessional bodies, and they are being challenged by the increasing number of united and uniting churches around the world. A number of critical questions need to be faced by the World Council and the World Confessional Families on the basis of their common calling to work for the renewal and unity of the churches for the sake of witnessing to the one, undivided Lord of the world. We have talked about this for so long without doing much that relations are in danger of becoming polite rather than cordial. I am more and more convinced that this matter needs to be given very serious attention in the coming years.

Ironically, in many cases, the WCC's relations with the largest non-member church, the Roman Catholic Church, have been far more intense than with many member churches. The Nairobi Assembly looked forward eagerly to the day "when it will be possible for the Roman Catholic Church to become a member of the WCC." The way forward is to multiply signs of a covenanted relationship between the World Council and its member churches and the Roman Catholic Church in all places.

I have given a good deal of space to the calling of the WCC to enable member churches to grow toward a truly ecumenical conciliar fellowship, because I believe passionately that it is the most crucial task before us, whatever programmes we adopt and carry out. Perhaps one of the most significant remarks made about the Nairobi Assembly was that of a Jewish rabbi who was present as a guest. He said that he had known many churches, but at Nairobi he experienced the reality of *the church*. I imagine that what he was referring to was the fact that the churches' representatives at Nairobi behaved as though they did share a covenanted fellowship, that they belonged to each other in suffering and joy, and were committed to their common Lord for the sake of the world. I covet this covenant relationship as a normal fact between the churches and the Council.

## *The incarnation of our faith*

The second guideline calls for programmes which will engage the churches in making a fuller common witness through a common understanding of the gospel and tradition and through an authentic incarnation of the Christian faith in each situation. Why do we have to emphasize this?

In the first place we are still unclear about the dynamic nature of our incarnate faith in Christ. Even the Programme Guidelines Committee at Nairobi fell into the traditional trap. It said:

> All programmes should be conceived and implemented in a way that engages the churches in the effort to reach a common understanding of the gospel and the tradition and under the guidance of the Holy Spirit to make possible a fuller common witness. At the same time there is need to search for an authentic incarnation of the Christian faith in the historic circumstances of a given place.

Note that the understanding of the gospel and tradition and of an authentic incarnation of the faith are seen as parallel rather than as simultaneous. The real debate about what mission and evangelism mean is whether we speak about faith *and* action, or faith *in* action and action *in* faith. The very term "word," *dabhar* in Hebrew, means not only word, but also act, happening, transaction. God's word is his act, and supremely so in the word made flesh in Christ. Action/reflection is not just a methodological tool for carrying out our work. It is rather an expression of the nature of our faith and of the obedience it demands. It should therefore be integral to all the programmes of the Council and of the member churches.

Second, we have been stressing recently that faith can only be expressed in the particularities of our existence. There are no dominant theological norms or confessions which can be applied everywhere. Nor can we expect to adopt an ecumenical confession of the faith which must be adopted everywhere. History, culture, locality must be taken seriously as the matrix of any incarnation of the faith. However, we have not yet found a way of devising the programmes of the Council or even of our own individual churches which will enable the many-sided grace and wisdom of God to be discerned through the many-sided particularities of persons, positions, and places. This affects the whole style in which we work as a Council and the ways in which we consult the churches, congregations, and communities and cooperate with them. Conciliar fellowship is meaningless unless it manifests the varied gifts in the different members of the body of Christ.

Third, we are not yet clear about our participation in dialogue with people of other faiths and ideologies. There are those who still demand a clear definition of dialogue before they will participate in it. This has led to inconclusive and sometimes acrimonious debates. But dialogue by its very character defies definition. It is a relationship, a meeting of life with life. Like love it can only be known if it is experienced. It is an act of faith, a giving of the blessing, a sharing with the other of all that we have received from God in Christ. It is also the recognition that in the inscrutable wisdom of God, the other has some blessing to bestow, some life and vitality from the depths of being. Christ is only betrayed when we deny ourselves of this outgoing, outpouring covenant blessing to the other and with the other. A Hindu guest in Nairobi spoke with astonishment about how the the Christian participants assumed the agonies of the world. He was implicitly saying that this is a distinctive element of Christianity. As the early Fathers of the church said: "That which is not assumed, taken up, cannot be redeemed." The emphasis on dialogue in community is another way of spelling out what the incarnation of our faith means.

### The struggle for true humanity

The third guideline, which calls us to ensure that all WCC programmes emphasize the Christian imperative to participate in the struggle for human dignity and social justice, does not need to be belaboured. The World Council has been and remains deeply and irrevocably committed to this struggle. What is new in this guideline is that it asks that *all* programmes of the Council should be so involved.

What I said about the first guideline is also relevant here. The covenant relationship we speak about among the churches within the World Council is without content and fruitless unless it is truly within God's purpose that all men and women, all races and peoples, should enter into that covenant and share the blessing. We are familiar with the promise of the new covenant, as told by the prophet Jeremiah:

> Behold, the days are coming, says the Lord, when I will make a new covenant with the house of Israel and the house of Judah.... I will put my law within them, and I will write it upon their hearts; and I will be their God, and they shall be my people. And no longer shall each man teach his neighbour and each his brother, saying, "Know the Lord," for they shall all know me, from the least of them to the greatest, says the Lord; for I will forgive their iniquity, and I will remember their sin no more (Jer. 31:31-34).

But what does Jeremiah mean by "knowing" the Lord? Earlier he attacks King Shallum, the son and successor of Josiah the reforming king:

> Do you think you are a king because your cedar is splendid? Did not your father eat and drink and do justice and righteousness? Then it was well with him. He judged the cause of the poor and needy; then it was well. Is not this to know me? says the Lord. But

you have eyes and heart only for your dishonest gain, for shedding innocent blood, and for practicing oppression and violence (Jer. 22:15-17).

"Knowing" in Hebrew means to be in the most intimate of relations with the other, to share one's being with the other. Knowing the Lord and knowing our fellow human beings made in his own image go hand in hand. Knowing the Lord means practicing justice and righteousness, upholding the cause of the poor and the oppressed, maintaining the integrity of God's purpose of good. It is the blessing in this cursed existence of ours in a divided, unjust world.

To be human is to be blessed, full of life, and to be a blessing, share life with others. To be inhuman is to be cursed, directionless, lifeless, and to be a curse, to separate from others, to deprive others of life. The ecumenical movement and the WCC exist to promote the human, the blessing, and to expose and exorcise the inhuman, the curse. The basis of the movement and of the Council is the confession of him who is truly human, Jesus Christ, who came to bless us with life in all its fullness.

It is therefore an integral function of the WCC to be involved deeply in the struggle for true humanity. We have a mandate to intensify our commitment to this struggle. We must commit ourselves to press courageously and persistently for the understanding and implementation of human rights, including religious liberty, in face of the increasing violation of those rights everywhere. In particular, we must continue to combat against racism, that dreadful curse which dehumanizes those who practice it and those who suffer from it. Similarly, the equally dehumanizing discrimination against women in church and society can no longer be tolerated by Christians, and every effort must be made to create living signs of a community of women and men in Christ. In Christ, we find our true humanity as belonging to the one family of God. Thus we participate in the covenant community promised to Abraham and in the blessing, the sharing, of the life of God.

In the last several years the WCC has sought to give a lead in pursuing the search for a just, participatory, and sustainable society, to expose those factors which hinder the growth of such a society, and explore those which promote it. Thus we analyze the power structures, created and strengthened particularly by transnational corporations, militarism, and the escalating arms race, which prevent a just international economic order from being developed. But we are even more challenged to act in solidarity with the poor and the oppressed in all lands and to be involved with them in programmes which encourage self-reliance and self-identity and enable them to become truly human communities.

As we read this catalogue of enormous challenges and tasks — many of which we shall look at in more detail later in this book — we are bound to feel the impossibility for human wit, skill, and resources to deal with them. But the glory of our biblical faith is that we are called to be a covenant fellowship of the people of God who "generate hope, reconciliation, liberation, and justice." We must deepen our resources of spiritual life, find new styles of living which emphasize what it means to be a blessing, and practice asceticism, a new discipline in our use of our natural and human resources for sustaining a life of meaning and grace. Spirituality so conceived is not an escape from the conflicts of our world, but rather the way to place ourselves in the fellowship of the Spirit, whose power and wisdom can enable and direct us to be bearers of the covenant blessing.

The ecumenical movement is always the time of testing in the wilderness, the pilgrim march towards the *oikoumene* to come (Heb. 2:5), with Christ as the pioneer and fulfilling force of our faith. It was in the wilderness that Israel entered into a covenant relationship with God and received the law, the teaching of the way of their just and merciful God, and the instructions as to how they should offer him a worthy worship. It was in the wilderness that they were tested by foes within and without. And there they also received the *manna*, the sustaining power of God to go on their pilgrim way. When our Lord began his ministry, conscious of his calling and of its cost, he went into the wilderness to face the agonizing test. We too are called, through this covenant fellowship within the World Council, to join the pilgrim way, whatever the cost, but always in the certainty of the enabling power, the blessing, of our risen Lord.

## The love of power and the power of love

To speak of divine power enabling and guiding us on our pilgrim way in the wilderness is an encouraging and comforting thought. But the history of the church to the present day shows all too many examples in which divine sanction has been claimed for the misuse of power and the wrong kind of power. We are well advised, therefore, to be cautious when we talk about power, mindful of the ambiguities inherent in this subject.

In what follows, I shall use the phrase "the power of love" as an expression pointing to the kingly rule of God in Christ over the *oikoumene* and to our calling to be messengers in word and deed of the kingly rule of God. "The love of power" is a convenient way of indicating its opposite.

The English word "power" comes from an old French word, today spelled *pouvoir*, a verb turned noun which meant, like its Latin equivalent *potere, posse*, and the noun *potentia*, "to be able, to have the possibility to do." Power is therefore not an unchangeable, measurable factor like "physical strength," "military might," or "Gross National Product." It isn't fixed. For example, in the days of the British raj in India the astonishing thing was that so few people could rule so vast and populated a country. Similarly, Mahatma Gandhi was able to mobilize great power in the people by nonviolent means and make nonsense of British rule in India.

Two things can be said about power. First, it is the capacity to initiate the new, to realize the possible, to change, to do the unexpected. As such it is an essentially human quality, the capacity to resist what threatens to destroy one's being and to extend or fulfil one's being. Secondly, power depends for its exercise on people's living together in word and deed and on their vocational consciousness. The power of the British raj was the collective sense of a destiny to extend the being of the British people to another people. On the other hand, Gandhi and his followers exercised power because of their will to self-affirmation, to liberate themselves from that which threatened their being, their potential as a people.

It is interesting to observe in history that tyranny, the concerted use of violence, depends on the isolation and separation of the the tyrant from his subjects, with the resultant isolation of the subjects from each other through mutual suspicion and fear. Divide and rule becomes the way of the tyrant. E. M. Forster's justly famous novel, *A Passage to India*, brings out that self-defeating element in the British raj. Such tyranny kills any capacity for change, for the really new. It becomes static, wooden, mechanical, and finally impotent and dead. We do not speak of "self-power," but of "self-control." "Self-power" is a contradiction in terms, because power depends on relationships, while self-control is the means by which one limits one's self-assertiveness for the sake of participating in the power of the group which responds to one's own sense of destiny, of self-fulfilment. Power is therefore essentially political, concerned with life together as people speak and act, seeking to fulfil their destiny as human beings.

In a penetrating analysis of power Hannah Arendt writes: "Power is actualized only where word and deed have not parted company, where words are not empty and deeds not brutal, where words are not used to veil intentions but to disclose realities, and deeds are not used to violate and destroy but to establish relations and create new realities" (*The Human Condition*). Such a splendid understanding of power points beyond power to a reality which acts as its aim and motivation. It is the actualization of something beyond the normal behaviour of people. It is this reality which we call love. Paul has admirably brought out the impotence of power without love in his immortal words:

> I may speak in tongues of men or of angels, but if I am without love, I am a sounding gong or a clanging cymbal. I may have the gift of prophecy, and know every hidden truth; I may have faith strong enough to move mountains; but if I have no love, I am nothing. I may dole out all I possess, or even give my body to be burnt, but if I have no love, I am none the better (1 Cor. 13:1-3).

Love, as Paul Tillich said, "is the ultimate power of union, the ultimate victory over separation." Love is the reunion of the separated, the isolated. The fundamental reality of our human existence is our separation from one another — a separation which belongs to our nature as persons and has been aggravated by the many walls of separation we build between one another both individually and collectively. This separation reveals itself in divisions of class and caste, of race, culture, and nation. Sometimes it results in, sometimes it is caused by a division within oneself, a lack of "centredness" and therefore the loss of power to achieve one's potentiality in relation to and in contact with others. Separation leads to impotence and death. Love is therefore the foundation of power, because power cannot flourish in separation. The human task is therefore how to conquer separation, how to work for reunion, for fullness of life, for the enthronement of love. But it is a task which humanity in its turbulent history has abundantly demonstrated to be beyond its capacity, because the real separation is between persons and communities and the ground of their being, God.

God is love, the First Epistle of John tells us, because he has deployed his power in his Son Jesus Christ to remove the obstacles which separate us from him and from other human beings — and this means life. This love was manifest in Christ's laying down his life for us (1 John 3:16). Receiving God's love and life, we are given his Spirit, his power, which both unites us to him through the acknowledgment of our fellowship with his Son and impels us to break down our separation from one another. God's love of us and our returning love of him propels us to our fellows, to a political life, to the exercise of power.

Hence love is a dwelling with one another by living with God. Loving others means recognizing the presence of God. The rabbis used to say: "Whenever a poor man is at your door, remember the Lord is beside him." Indeed, the Hebrew word Yahweh, translated "Lord" in many English versions, means "he who is present." It is no surprise that when the rabbis interpreted Leviticus 19:18, "You shall love your neighbour as yourself: I am the Lord," they translated "I am the Lord" by the phrase, "I am he who is there." Equally significant is the Hebrew meaning of the words "as yourself," that is, "as you are, made in the image of God." We are reminded of Jesus' familiar words concerning the unveiling of the kingdom of God and the judgment on the *oikoumene*: "Anything you did for one of my brothers here, however humble, you did it for me" (Matt. 25:40). This means a quickened and sensitive perception of others so as to remove all that separates them from themselves and others. Seeing others in love means seeing God — the hungry, the thirsty, the stranger, the naked, the imprisoned in body or spirit. Charles Raven recalls that John Oman once said: "When I speak of a Christian I mean a person with whom to see is to act." Nietzsche, in one of his flashes of profound insight, exclaimed: "Where shall we find justice, which is love with seeing eyes?" Those who really see and act have that perfect love which dispels fear (1 John 4:18). "Perfect" in its Hebrew background means "all-including." When Jesus says: "You shall be perfect as your heavenly Father is perfect" (Matt. 5:48), it comes as the climax of his teaching on the all-including love and goodness of God:

> You have learned that they were told, "Love your neighbour, hate your enemy." But what I tell you is this: Love your enemies and pray for your persecutors; only so can you be children of your heavenly Father, who makes his sun to rise on good and bad alike, and sends the rain on the honest and the dishonest. If you love only those who love you, what reward can you expect? Surely the tax-gatherers do as much as that. And if you greet only your brothers, what is there extraordinary about that? Even the heathen do as much (Matt. 5:43-47).

Fear comes from a life of separation, of excluding and being excluded. Fear results in one's closing oneself in and becoming powerless to be oneself and to speak and act creatively. It carries its own judgment of death rather than life. There is a further thought which John discloses about love. Unless there is a unity of speaking and acting, there is no love, no communion with God and man. "If a man says, 'I love God,' while hating his brother, he is a liar" (1 John 4:20). "The kingdom of God," Paul told the factious Corinthians, "is not a matter of talk, but of power" (1 Cor. 4:20). Thus love is nothing natural to human beings, and yet it is the indispensable requirement for any meaningful existence. Only in God is love possible. That is why it is a command, a summons to actualize our potential for making real the unity of the *oikoumene*. Love is an inescapable task. Dietrich Bonhoeffer, in an unfinished chapter of his *Ethics*, sums up this love which is of God as follows:

> Love, therefore, is the name for what God does to man in over-coming the disunion in which man lives. This deed of God is Jesus Christ, is reconciliation. And so love is something which happens to man, something passive, something over which he does not himself dispose, simply because it lies beyond his existence in disunion. Love means the undergoing of the transformation of one's entire existence by God; it means being drawn in into the world as it lives and must live before God and in God. Love, therefore, is not man's choice, but is the election of man by God.

Many of the realities we have to deal with in the World Council of Churches arise from the denial of love and demand from us the utmost exercise of the power of love. Countless examples illustrate the tragic separation which grips the *oikoumene* today, and we must come to terms with their pervasive demonic character. Paul calls them "the principalities and powers," which seem to control persons and societies and reduce them to the impotence of blind and senseless oppression and violence or helpless despair.

There is of course the tragic reality of southern Africa, where colonial and racial oppression has become institutionalized and the whole legal, economic, political, and even religious structure is directed to one aim — the separation of whites from blacks — in a manner which deprives the blacks of any meaningful existence.

Latin America offers other examples. Nations under tyrannical rule are rushing into economic growth with the active support of Western capital. But the human costs are frightful. The system is based on vast estates in the hands of the few, while the majority are deprived and dispossessed, treated as objects rather than subjects. Those who seek to overcome this institutionalized violence are ruthlessly suppressed or expelled. In the name of fighting world Communism, the so-called "national security doctrine" justifies the most horrible crimes against defenseless people.

Or one could refer to the Middle East. Some years ago I attended a meeting of Christians concerned about biblical perspectives on the problem of the Middle East. An unusual thing took place — a dialogue between an Israeli youth leader and a young Palestinian leader. Both described the agony their peoples have suffered through history — a suffering in which the Christian world has played its part. One in their suffering, they found themselves caught in a gulf of mutual fear and mistrust which, since 1948, has led Arabs and Israelis into recurring bouts of war and violence. As Martin Buber said, "There is no salvation save through the renewal of the dialogical relation, and this means, above all, through the overcoming of existential mistrust." To this depressing list of situations one could add the tragic irony of Eastern Europe, where a revolutionary effort at overcoming these separations has led to new forms of separation and oppression. One could even remark that the experience of the socialist states has encouraged people to despair and opt out of the struggle for change, because of the lack of a human face to socialism as officially practiced in those countries.

What all this adds up to is that the human family has reached a crucial stage. Are we going to continue acquiescing in this situation and wait in resignation for disaster to overtake us all? Or are we going to escape into privatist or parochial exclusiveness? Or shall we take the position, so tempting to pacifists like myself, that our first concern must be to keep our hands pure and undefiled from the ambiguities and compromises of political engagement, while contenting ourselves with individual or collective good works here and there? Or shall we be daring enough to take with radical seriousness our calling to enter into the struggle for a just society and to demonstrate in word and deed the power of love?

Some penetrating questions are addressed to those attracted by the pacifist position in a World Council of Churches statement on "Violence and Nonviolence in the Struggle for Justice":

— Are you taking with sufficient seriousness the tenacity and depth of violence in the structures of society, and the social disruption its diminution is likely to require?

— May nonviolent action emasculate effective resistance at crucial points in a struggle?

— In adhering to this as an absolute principle are you not in danger of giving the means (nonviolence, i.e. reduced revolutionary violence) priority over the end sought (justice, i.e. reduced structural violence)?

— Are you more concerned with your own "good" conscience than with the good of the oppressed?

On the basis of a biblical understanding of love, what can "the power of love" mean for us? I would suggest three elements to the power of love in action: listening, giving, and forgiving.

*Listening* is the process by which we recognize the other person or persons as sharing a common life together with us. It is the way of dialogue, the sharing of life with life, mutual respect. Listening means seeing the other, eye to eye and mouth to mouth, being open to learn, to be informed, to be judged, to know, to communicate with each other. Listening, learning, communicating — here is love in word and act overcoming the barriers of existential mistrust. South Africa, Latin America, the Middle East, Eastern Europe — these are not disagreeable realities to which we close our eyes. They are part of our life, and woe to us if we do not allow ourselves to know them fully, to live in and with them until the separation burns into our very beings and becomes so intolerable that we must let all others know that we and they may act. But to do this we shall have to overcome our normal arrogance, our habit of treating people as objects rather than as subjects, of being selective and exclusive in our actions, or of imagining that we can overcome separation without the full participation of the separated.

A few months before he was murdered, Eduardo Mondlane, the leader of the Mozambique Liberation Movement (FRELIMO), told me of a conversation he had had with Che Guevara, the famous Argentine revolutionary. Che offered his services to fight against the Portuguese, arguing that one task which could be undertaken was the overthrow of Portuguese colonial power. Mondlane countered that involving his people in awareness of who they were and preparing themselves for the constructive tasks of building up a just society through their active participation was an equally important task. Che Guevara regarded this as a waste of effort, and he went off to Bolivia with a small band of élite friends. They fought in the mountains against the oppressive government forces on behalf of the peasants, but having little contact with them. In the end, Che was betrayed by the uncomprehending and scared peasants and shot. He had failed to understand that listening, learning, sharing are indispensable prerequisites for mobilizing the potential of people for newness and change, essential elements of the power of love.

*Giving* is certainly an often-recognized element of love as a power of overcoming separation and disunion. But much depends on what we understand by giving. Earlier we quoted Paul: "I may dole out all I possess, or even give my body to be burnt (some manuscripts read: even seek glory by self-sacrifice), but if I have no love, I am none the better" (1 Cor. 13:3). "The gift without the giver is bare." How much of the charity offered by churches and other agencies through the years has been real *caritas,* caring? T.S. Eliot wrote in *Murder in the Cathedral* of

> Pride drawing sustenance from impartiality,
> Pride drawing sustenance from generosity.

And again,

> The last temptation is the greatest treason:
> To do the right deed for the wrong reason...
> Sin grows with doing good.

Eliot saw that "impartiality" and "generosity" suggest a lack of total commitment; indeed, that there is an "impartiality" which is in fact partial, which lacks the quality of all-including involvement.

Giving is of no value unless it is part of the listening, learning, sharing attitude. Giving has no power unless we are willing to receive. Before going to Haiti in 1950 to work among the poor peasants I saw the film *Monsieur Vincent,* about the remarkable seventeenth-century French priest Vincent de Paul. Before his death, he told a recruit of the Daughters of Charity, "It is only by your love that the poor will forgive you for your loaf of bread and your bowl of soup."

The only giving which works for the reunion of the separated is that which carries with it the cry of crucifixion: "My God, my God, why hast thou forsaken me?" Only when we allow ourselves to experience the full force of separation, by being fully with the separated, can we become instruments of reconciliation. It is in the weakness of self-giving that the power of love can release the healing, reconciling love of God.

*Forgiving* is the most searching test of the power of love. Power, the capacity to do something new, unexpected, creative, as part of our inescapable relations with others, and love, self-giving for others, are most signally manifest in forgiving. In Old English, the prefix "for" implied intensive force, something done in excess, through and through, overwhelmingly, overpoweringly. "Forgive" therefore means to give through and through with overwhelming power. What is natural to human beings is vengeance, returning injury for injury, violence for violence, oppression for oppression, hatred for hatred. It is not an action, but a reaction. Instead of creating and affirming life, it is destructive and life-denying.

The nerve of the gospel is that in our impotence and deathly existence, God in his freedom and almighty power has entered into our lot in the flesh and blood of his Son in self-giving love. He has given himself utterly, through and through, with overwhelming power for our release, our liberation, and through us for the liberation of the whole creation (Rom. 8:18-22). In his ministry, we see him listening to, sharing the lot of, and communicating with the poor and the oppressed, and with the rich and the oppressors. We see him giving himself in acts of healing, creative power. We see his love being displayed with relentless clarity as he exposes the conscious and unconscious selfishness of human beings.

We see it most clearly in his crucifixion — a political act accomplished in the public place of Golgotha. And in the agony of the cross he prayed: "Father, *forgive* them, for they know not what they do."

We are identified with those who crucified and crucify him afresh; and, if we have learned to listen and to give, we too are identified with him in his groan of separation from God. Only thus can we be forgiven, released again and again from our separation from God and from each other, and made anew in the power of his risen life to be reconciled and enlisted in his reconciling work. Only thus can we be enabled to share his burning wrath against the separations caused by human sinfulness and his unwearying compassion for sinners.

Forgiveness is the clearest evidence of the power of love. It means, as Tillich put it so forcefully in one of his sermons,

> reconciliation in spite of estrangement; reunion in spite of hostility; acceptance of those who are unacceptable; and reception of those who are rejected.... Forgiveness is the answer, the divine answer, to the question implied in our existence.... He who is forgiven knows what it means to love God. And he who loves God is also able to accept life and to love it.

Thus forgiveness gives us the possibility of starting afresh and beginning something new. As Paul put it, "When anyone is united to Christ, there is a new world, a new act of creation; the old order has gone, the old life is over; and a new order, a new life has already begun" (2 Cor. 5:17).

A clear alternative is placed before us — the love of power, which produces and maintains separation, leading to death; or the power of love, which travails for the breaking down of separation and for the reunion of the *oikoumene*, that we may all share the endless life of the open city. The power of love is hope in action — action founded on the divine promise: "Behold, I am making all things new."

# 5. Toward an ecumenical life-style

We have been speaking in rather general terms in the preceding chapters of the challenges raised by the gospel and the resources which the Christian faith promises and provides for those who respond to its call. Throughout we have been emphasizing, from various angles, that what Paul calls "working out our salvation" inevitably involves us in an attitude of openness to the whole world and its problems and can never be a matter of individual achievement. The covenant fellowship of the ecumenical movement represents, in its ups and downs, successes and failures, an effort to face this challenge in the world of today.

Now we shall be looking in somewhat more detail at a number of specific areas in which the ecumenical movement — particularly through the World Council of Churches — has sought to help the churches work together in our world. We shall do so not only with an eye on the past but also with a view to the future of the ecumenical movement. In focusing on an organization and the events and trends in its history, we must not allow the human side of the story so to predominate that we lose sight of the deeper realities in which the ecumenical movement has been anchored.

Earlier we observed that the ecumenical movement in this century has been motivated by the prayer of our Lord that we all may be one. As he and the Father shared a co-inherent life, so we may share this life with him and the Father and with each other, so that the world may believe. From the start, the ecumenical movement has thus been not a man-made association of like-minded people, but a response to God's revelation of himself in Christ through the Holy Spirit. A driving force in the movement in the early days was fellowship in prayer, later epitomized in the Week of Prayer for Christian Unity. The movement was also anchored in the revelation through the word of God in the Scripture and the witness to this revelation of the Godhead in the tradition of the church. However differently all this has been appropriated and expressed during the years, there can be no doubt that the ecumenical movement has been understood and lived out of the life and calling of the blessed Trinity.

All this was grasped dynamically, not as a static theological fact, but in obedience to the challenge and call of God in historical situations. The 1910 World Missionary Conference took place in the context of the missionary movement of Western churches to countries where other faiths reigned. But it took place at a time of Western colonial and imperialist expansion. The divisive and competing ways in which the gospel was being proclaimed were a scandal which obscured the real scandal of the gospel. This missionary movement exposed the centuries-old divisions of the churches and pushed them back to the source of their life in the Trinity. During and after World War I it was the terrible way in which Christians slaughtered each other in the name of national allegiances and ideologies which forced the churches to face their lack of credibility as instruments of God's reconciling work in Christ. The Life and Work and Faith and Order Movements were the fruit of this sharpened awareness.

These well-known facts suggest an important point about the future of the ecumenical movement. One might say that the "text" on which the ecumenical movement is based is the revelation of the Trinity, while the "context," by which the movement is animated and driven forward, is the storms of world history. It is essential to remember this, because criticisms of the present state of the ecumenical movement are often made by people who judge the movement out of a particular period or influence and not out of the dynamic realities of God's *energeia*, his operation and action, in the ongoing movement of history.

*Facing the future*

In the course of the thirty-odd years since the formation of
the World Council of Churches, all the main streams of the
Christian community have been drawn into the ecumenical
movement. In 1948 the Council was a world council only in
name. Most of the Orthodox churches did not or could not
respond to the invitation to become member churches. Most of
the churches in what is now called the Third World were still
under the tutelage of the Western churches. The Roman
Catholic Church remained aloof. Today the World Council has
in its fellowship the Orthodox, Anglican, Protestant, and Pente-
costal traditions; and the Roman Catholic Church has become
a living part of the ecumenical movement. Moreover, the
churches have been in conversation with each other and have
joined locally, nationally, regionally, and internationally in various ways in order to learn from each other and witness
together. Although we tend to take all this for granted, this has
been no mean achievement in so short a time, given the many
centuries of hostility, mistrust, and fear of one another. We do
not often enough rejoice and give thanks that God has drawn
his people together in this miraculous way, using such instruments as the World Council of Churches.

We should pause here to note briefly the special contribution
which the Orthodox Churches have made to the ecumenical
movement. With their constant affirmation that they represent
the one unbroken church of the triune God, they have kept the
primacy and urgency of the issues of unity before the other
churches. They have reminded the churches of the Reformation
of the trinitarian basis of our faith and helped others discern
afresh the wealth of the divine revelation and the economy of
God and our own calling to reproduce that richness in the relation between human beings and creation. The patristic concept
of *theosis* as the goal of the revelation of the Trinity — that
humanity and creation be filled with the divine life — gives us
rich clues for dealing with some of today's burning issues.

Since 1948 there have been great advances in our thinking
and action on the four major emphases of the ecumenical
movement — unity, mission, renewal, and service. The driving
force of the ecumenical movement has undoubtedly been the
call to unity in faith and order. We have moved from getting

acquainted with each other as church traditions to rethinking in fresh terms the issues which divide us. The goal of the unity we seek was articulated by the Fifth Assembly in Nairobi: "To call the churches to the goal of visible unity in one faith and in one eucharistic fellowship expressed in worship and in common life in Christ, and to advance towards that unity in order that the world may believe." The same Assembly also commended another expression of the unity we seek: "The one Church is to be envisioned as a *conciliar fellowship* of local churches which are themselves truly united. In this conciliar fellowship, each local church possesses, in communion with the others, the fullness of catholicity, witnesses to the same apostolic faith, and therefore recognises the others as belonging to the same Church of Christ and guided by the same Spirit." To this is added a concern that the unity of the church be directly related to God's purpose to unite all people and all things in Christ. The unity of the church is the sign and sacrament of the unity of humankind. All those things which divide human beings need to be redeemed, and this redeemed life needs to be manifest in the body of Christ as the new humanity. So the issues of racial and sexual discrimination, of economic, social, and political injustice, and of deprivation of any kind are the inescapable context within which we must seek our unity in the divine triunity.

Perhaps the most significant achievement of the search for unity has been the attempt to reach a consensus on baptism, the eucharist, and the ministry, an effort in which Orthodox, Roman Catholic, Anglican, and Protestant Christians have engaged. It is hoped that by the Sixth Assembly in 1983 statements on these will be presented for transmission to the churches. One issue for the future will be how the churches will receive and act on such consensus statements from their varied traditions.

Mission and evangelism have been a central concern of the ecumenical movement from the beginning. The issue of proselytism has been faced, and statements and agreements have been made which enable the churches to go beyond condemning proselytism to undertaking joint action for mission. They are seeking prayerfully to discover together what God is calling them to do in particular places, to measure their resources for meeting the tasks, and to find ways of acting together or for each other. This is seen in such activities as urban and industrial mission, ministerial formation, education, medical and social work, lay training. Furthermore, mission and evangelism have come increasingly to be seen as the essential task of each congregation. Great themes of the church's mission — salvation, the kingdom of God, hope — have been and are being affirmed and communicated in different cultures and situations.

Dialogue with persons who do not profess the Christian faith is being conducted in an attitude of mutual respect and openness, which in many places has transformed the relations of Christians with people of other faiths, and has helped Christians rediscover some of the hidden riches of their own faith. In a world in which people hunger for a sense of meaning, the churches are called to find ways to proclaim by word and deed the varied riches of the faith as grasped in different cultures and to be open to the working of the Holy Spirit for the life of the world.

The renewal of the churches for unity and mission has also become an accepted fact among us. In an earlier period there was a great deal of talk about the need to mobilize the laity in the life and witness of the church in the world — men and women, old and young, as the priesthood of all believers manifesting the divine life at home, at school, at work, and in all our relationships. Since then the role of the laity in the worship and life of the churches has been changing, and we have been rethinking our educational processes so that those who are being taught are treated as participants in the process of learning, who have something to offer, even if it is only new ways of asking questions.

Service to the world has always been seen as an obligation of the churches. Certainly, since World War II the churches have been active in mobilizing massive aid to people in need, whatever their nation, creed, or race. They have been helping refugees and have been attentive to the needs of the poor and the oppressed. On the basis of the gospel they have been a voice for those who had no voice and have proclaimed the convictions on which a just and peaceful society can be built and maintained. During these years the churches have been forced beyond making general statements and giving assistance to people in need to getting at the causes of war, poverty, and the conflicts which grip our world. On the issues of racism, sexism, violations of political, economic, personal, and social rights, the arms race and disarmament, ideologies, and options for a more just society, the churches have found themselves divided. These divisions run right across ecclesiastical traditions. Although the ecumenical fellowship has been profoundly strained by these clashing views, there has been at least one great gain: the churches can no longer be dismissed as ghettoes, identified with the status quo or the side of the oppressors. There have been the beginnings of a distinct disengagement with the secular powers. This, too, is a challenge which the churches will continue to face together in the future, because the powers cannot tolerate the questioning of their policies and actions. Violations of religious liberty are taking new and more ominous forms in today's world. This will be a vital concern of the ecumenical movement in the coming years. Certainly, through the ecumenical movement the churches and Christians have been able to be engaged in the world more relevantly for the sake of the gospel, even though this engagement has brought about stresses and strains.

Not least important in this period has been the way the churches and Christians have been thinking afresh about science and technology and the transformation of our world being achieved by them. Science and technology have greatly changed the relations of people and nature, and of nations with each other. Given the earlier hostility of the churches to science, we have made great strides in our reflections during these thirty years. Scientists and technologists are now raising with Christians profound questions about creation and about human responsibility in the use of nature and of the resources of the earth. Here again, events have pushed the churches to recover a theology of creation which grows out of our faith in the triune God, who is Creator, Redeemer, Sustainer, and Perfector. There will be a great deal to think and do together in the coming years in this critical area, which both threatens the survival of the world and yet holds out exciting possibilities for creating a more just and sustainable society.

Any sober assessment of the past thirty years of thinking and living together in the ecumenical movement would conclude that one of the great difficulties has been that the insights we

have gained during these crowded and eventful years have been
too many and have come too fast for our churches to digest and
make their own. They have not become an integral part of the
life and thinking of the churches and therefore of their participation in the ecumenical movement. That is the crisis of the
ecumenical movement and the cause of the frustration of so
many who have been actively engaged in it. Without overlook-
ing the miracles of grace which God is performing as churches
around the globe discover each other and witness together, we
must nevertheless acknowledge that our churches have not
come to terms with all that we have been learning in the ecumenical movement. If there is to be a future for the ecumenical
movement, we shall have to face this issue head on. How can
the *whole* people of God discover what we might describe as an
ecumenical life-style? How can they come more fully to participate in the ecumenical movement, listening to one another,
sharing each other's insights and experiences, and entering into
ever widening and deeper relationships for the sake of living
and witnessing to the gospel in today's world?

Clearly there are no easy answers to such questions. The miracles of grace, the signs of hope, the new insights that sustain an
"ecumenical life-style" emerge from the work of the Spirit
among people who are willing to make a commitment, a
response of faith. All the sermons preached and speeches made
and pages printed since 1948 — indeed, since long before that
— can only help the whole people of God to the extent that
they find a resonance in those who hear and read them. The
vision that stimulates an ecumenical life-style is not the product
of clever reasoning or shrewd public relations or slick sales-
manship. As we take a closer look at some of the dominant
themes on the present ecumenical agenda, it is well to bear this
limitation in mind.

## The mission of God

No one would deny that mission has always been at the heart
of the ecumenical movement. At the same time, it has been the
source of great controversy and disagreement, within churches,
within the ecumenical movement, and in the world at large. The
Latin phrase *missio Dei* has become current in the last several
years as a means of redefining what is meant by mission today.

Quite simply — and quite profoundly — what this phrase means to assert is that *mission is God's, not ours.* This fundamental truth was expressed with force and eloquence twenty years ago at the last full assembly of the International Missionary Council in Ghana, prior to the IMC's joining the WCC.

> The Christian world mission is Christ's, not ours. Prior to all our efforts and activities, prior to all our gifts of service and devotion, God sent His Son into the world. And He came in the form of a servant — a servant who suffered even to the death of the Cross.... We have seen it to be the only true motive of Christian mission and the only standard by which the spirit, method and modes of Christian missionary organization must be judged. We believe it is urgent that this word of judgment and mercy should be given full freedom to cleanse and redeem our present activities, lest our human pride in our activities hinder the free course of God's mission in the world.

Since that meeting in Ghana we have been trying to understand the significance of this insight for the participation of the church as the people of God in this mission. What have we discovered together?

In the first place, the God of the Bible is a missionary God, a God who *sends.* Through his word and Spirit, he creates man and woman in his own image and sends them out to master creation under his just and merciful will. He sends Abraham to be the sign of the new person of faith and obedience and the means of drawing broken humanity together. He sends Moses to call the people of Israel out of slavery into a new covenant, and he sends Israel as his people into the world to draw the other peoples into the circle of his covenant grace. He sends the prophets to deepen human understanding of his nature and purpose. Above all, he sends his Son to become a man among us and to reveal what it is to be human according to his design. He sends his Holy Spirit to make Christ's mission understood and effective in the world. Finally, he sends the apostles through the Son and the Spirit to the ends of the earth and to the end of time to carry out his mission.

Furthermore, this missionary God has chosen to act in history. "God so loved the world that he sent his only Son...," says John, though he goes on to say how hostile this world is to God and his will. But God's love for this world is revealed in his purpose to transform the world — a transformation shown in the life, death, and resurrection of Jesus Christ. This purpose embraces God's action in creation and redemption — with a fully responsible human partner sharing his lordship over creation in justice and peace. In Christ this new humanity has come into being, and the objective of this mission is that all should share in it. This biblical message is expressed very explicitly in Paul's letters, especially in Romans 8 and in Ephesians. Creation and history can only reach their fulfilment and goal in the human race, the crown of creation, God's true partner in the dialogue which is history.

The preparatory commission of the World Council's Fourth Assembly in Uppsala (1968) formulated this historical connection and its implications very sharply:

> The context of his sending is always history, since it is his concern to be present in the actual life situation of every man. Participation in God's mission is therefore entering into partnership with God in history, because our knowledge of God in Christ compels us to affirm that God is working out his purpose in the midst of the world and its historical processes. As God leads history out of the old into the new, he creates hope, in the sense of an active expectation of good in the transformation of the world for Christ's sake. Christians therefore understand the changes in history in the perspective of the mission of God and so, trusting in God's promises, they dare to risk involving themselves in actual history, ever ready to adopt new forms of responsibility for the world.

In the third place, the idea that the mission is God's sharpens our focus on the gospel as the good news of renewed humanity in Christ. The Uppsala documents, while recognizing that the New Testament uses several messianic images in speaking about God's mission, lifted up humanization as the goal of mission.

> We believe that more than others it communicates in our period of history the meaning of the messianic goal. In another time the goal of God's redemptive work might best have been described in terms of man turning towards God rather than in terms of God turning towards men. Today the fundamental question is much more that of *true* man, and the dominant concern of the missionary congregation must therefore be to point to the humanity in Christ as the goal of mission.

The Bible expresses the same reality of the new humanity in the word *shalom*, peace. The goal towards which God is working, the ultimate end of his mission, is the establishment of *shalom*. This involves the realization of the full potentialities of all creation and its ultimate reconciliation and unity in Christ.

Let me enumerate four consequences of these central insights. In the first place, the church as the people of God is not the centre and goal of mission, but the means and instrument. The church participates in God's mission, in what God is doing in his world, but the church cannot be above Christ, its head, who came as a servant and surrendered his life for the salvation of the world. As Christ took the form or structure proper to God's purpose, so the church must adapt its forms and structures to God's mission today as during every period in history.

Such an understanding of mission obliges us to reconsider three attitudes very common in all our churches: (a) the tendency to equate the church with the kingdom of God, rather than to see it as a sign of the kingdom; (b) the tendency, by speaking of "our mission," to force those whom we seek to evangelize into *our* patterns of thinking and living; and (c) the tendency to regard our historically conditioned structures as fixed and sacred and indispensable for the fulfilment of God's mission.

Second, if the drama of mission is God's engagement with the world, the church must take with radical seriousness what is happening in that world. Mission may not mean giving the church's answers to its own questions. It is of course true that the church is the messenger of God's questions to humanity and of his answer in Christ. But Christ himself showed deep concern for listening to people's questions before he deepened those questions and gave his answer in word and deed. We express this fundamental reality by saying that we must listen to the world's agenda. That is not just fashionable talk; as Uppsala pointed out, it means that Christians must "ask truly pertinent questions until the fullest meaning behind the world's agenda becomes perceptible for both world and Church. When this takes place, a movement from communication to communion has been initiated."

A third consequence of the conception of mission we have outlined is that the whole world is the mission field, not just what have traditionally been called non-Christian countries. The new humanity which is God's missionary purpose is the quest of every continent and country. All societies and communities, including those where Christians are dominant, are challenged and judged by God's word. Rebellion against God's will runs right across all cultures and societies.

Fourth, the church which participates in God's mission as the servant Body of Christ and takes the world's agenda seriously is itself being renewed to be the sign of the new humanity. The church as the people of God never remains static in the process of mission. Mission is not only concerned with the conversion of others but with the conversion of God's people. As they engage in God's mission to the world, they discover with ever greater depth their involvement in the tragedy of the world's disobedience and rebellion and their need for turning to God and receiving afresh his renewing grace.

At this moment of history the very survival of humanity is a priority on the world's agenda. At issue here are not primarily structures and systems, intellectual and technical skills, but the human beings who create and operate them. The focus is on humanity, on men and women, singly and corporately. Because that is precisely what our common biblical faith is about, the recognition that the Christian church has an inescapable responsibility for the survival of humanity is utterly fundamental. We can — indeed we must — make some brief and clear affirmations in this connection — the heart of a missionary faith:

(1) We believe in God the Father Almighty, Creator of heaven and earth. He created this one earth as an interdependent whole and man, male and female, to exercise mastery over it for good, that is, for mutual well-being in justice. The Old Testament prophetic tradition gives eloquent emphasis to this basic reality of our existence. Life before and with God means practicing justice and being devoted to loyal kindness to all.

(2) We believe in Jesus Christ who was made man in order to show us how human beings can practice this justice and show this kindness to the poor, the oppressed, the alienated, as expressions of life in and with God. To this end he challenges us to repentance, a radical change in our thinking, our attitudes,

indeed, our whole beings. Such repentance is an act of sharing in the death and resurrection of Christ — the crucifixion of our selfish existence and the affirmation of the impossible becoming real. Faith in the crucified and risen Lord is, there-fore, a radical break from a static understanding of our exis-tence into a dynamic living and daring God's future. Thomas Münzer, a Christian radical of the sixteenth century, said, "faith gives us the possibility of attempting and accomplishing the things which seem impossible." Charles Wesley put the same thought in verse:

> Faith, mighty faith, the promise sees,
>  And looks to that alone;
> Laughs at impossibilities,
>  And cries: It shall be done!

The great Danish Christian philosopher Søren Kierkegaard speaks of one who has faith as having "the passion of the pos-sible." Faith in Christ is a ferment making us new men and new women called to join in God's process of creating a new order in which justice prevails. To have faith is to hope and to act in hope. Such faith liberates us to struggle for a shared life in com-munity.

(3) We believe in the Holy Spirit, who is God's continuing presence with us in Christ. This Spirit is the creative power of a new age through the community of faith, the church which is the Body of Christ. In this body, animated by the Spirit, all the members, while having different functions, belong to each other. What the apostle Paul meant by this image is that both the difference and the belongingness are held together. When one member of the body suffers, all suffer with it. As a Zulu proverb says: "When a thorn gets into the toe, the whole body stoops to pick it out." But belief in the Holy Spirit also demands being open to the new and surprising in God's pur-pose, being carried forward by love into being signs of God's kingly rule and his justice. We are not our own but God's, and therefore we belong together as the human family.

On this simple but profound trinitarian basis, the church has no choice but to respond to God's mission. The church is *sent* to fulfil his creation. Negatively put, this means working for the survival of humanity. Positively, it means entering into the struggle for fullness of life in justice and peace. What then are the tasks before us?

In the first place, the Christian community has a primary responsibility to become much more intelligently informed about the threats to human survival and what is needed to create a new climate of thinking toward structures which can allow for and enhance the possibilities of human survival and fulfilment. One urgent task is educating the public about these issues from the perspective of our Christian faith. Of course, no such effort to draw people away from ignorance, indifference, fear, or hopelessness will succeed if we ourselves are not open to an imaginative grasp of our situation in its global and interdependent dimensions and determined to tackle the problems with faith, hope, and love.

Second, but by no means less important, the churches must set an example. What this means is examining our own life and structures to see in what ways we are participating in those forces which threaten the survival of mankind. Our devotion to the status quo, our dependence on an exploitative economic system, our tendency to settle for — indeed, indulge in — remedial acts of charity rather than tackling the root causes of injustice: all this must be called in question. We as churches cannot call the world to change its structures without ourselves demonstrating this in our worldwide fellowship.

Third, the churches must recognize a responsibility to support agencies and groups and persons of good will working for a new economic order. This support will be credible only when we devote our own resources and skills to assisting the poorest in both rich and poor countries to become conscious of their situation, self-reliant in their decision-making, and sensitive to the use of appropriate technology in developing themselves in social justice.

The churches' responsibility for the survival of humanity will be exercised in the ways in which we make the radical character of the gospel credible in concrete ways: simplicity of living, emphasizing the quality of life rather than the quantity of possessions, sharing resources of mind, skills, and funds, fearlessly challenging all that denies our human solidarity — all in the hope which is apparent in the certainty of the fulfilment of God's purpose for creation — his mission on which we are sent.

## The evangelizing church

Closely linked with the theme of *missio Dei* is the call to evangelize. It has always been a given of ecumenical thinking that the *raison d'être* of the church as the whole people of God is evangelization. It is not only the task of specialists, societies, religious orders, but of the whole Christian community. Only gradually is this view of the church being comprehended. But our experience in the ecumenical movement has shown that when churches in a local situation become deeply committed to evangelization in all its dimensions, they are driven to hear and begin to act on the prayer of our Lord "that they may all be one that the world may believe."

Our common concern for evangelization today demands that we discern the signs of the times. Historically, the church has always spoken of the *praeparatio evangelica*, the necessary preparation in the hearts of those to whom the gospel is addressed. Part of this process involves the discernment by the church of the way things are in the world today. What are some of these signs?

(1) Everywhere the process of secularization is going on. Through science and technology people are liberating themselves from the forces of nature and gaining their God-given dominion over it in order to become truly responsible for their existence rather than simply surrendering to fate. No longer is the world seen as closed and unchangeable but open to the future and in constant transformation. This development has not happened automatically. It is the result of biblical teaching and understanding. The whole biblical tradition is secular in purpose, enabling people whose faith is in the God of time and history to dethrone nature as an unknown, capricious god, and to come of age, as Bonhoeffer expressed it. Incredible advances in the conquest of space and vastly expanded means of transportation and communication have made the world a global village. Science and technology are providing new possibilities for conquering disease, dispelling ignorance, maintaining the human species. We can even plan ahead and mobilize resources to achieve our material designs. More than ever in history we are members one of another, neighbours sharing a common destiny.

We as Christians have been more adept at describing the other side of this development. We are aware of the new material gods to which people have given their allegiance — devotion to things, to having and consuming more and more, to using their enhanced power to increase war and destruction through armaments. Our global village is the scene of vicious divisions more deadly than ever before in history, of the greedy draining of our natural resources and the devastation of our environment. Such threats to our very survival as a species are contrived by human beings, and we carry inescapable responsibility for them in all our societies.

(2) Another sign of the times is the search of millions of people for ways to make life more humane. Everywhere there is a struggle for liberation from injustice of every kind — from structures which imprison and warp oppressors and oppressed alike; from the idolatry of ideological and social systems which resist change; from the faceless men and women who manipulate societies without having to be accountable; from the loss of purpose in work, leisure, or social relations; from the violation of human rights in all our countries; from the paralysis of recurrent world monetary crises and uncontrollable inflation which make nonsense of people's capacity to manage their own creations; and from the resulting apathy, cynicism, alienation, despair, and senseless violence.

This struggle for justice and community also finds its source in the biblical tradition. According to the Bible the structures of society are not fixed ends in themselves, but must be subject to God's purpose that they be spheres in which people can fulfil their destiny to live a shared life in community. The awareness by millions of submerged people of this destiny is one of the new facts of our time. The ruthless attempts to suppress this awareness through political and economic clout increase the human tragedy.

These two signs that people are coming of age by being more responsible for themselves *vis-à-vis* nature and the structures of society give rise to other signs of the times.

(3) Scientists, technologists, and other savants are asking fundamental questions about their responsibility for what they produce or are asked to produce. Gone are the days when these intellectuals saw their task in neutral Promethean terms. The

pertinence of these new questions is matched by the inadequacy of present theological categories for dealing with them. Indeed, the scientists and planners of societies are now speaking of the need for a new asceticism with regard to developing and sharing the world's resources.

(4) Those who have embraced or live under the ideological system of scientific materialism now recognize that the aim of a classless, just society is far from being achieved. In fact, the revolutionary termination of the oppression of feudalism and uncaring capitalism has been replaced by the regimentation of people into industrial development with little regard for human freedom and participation, resulting in new forms of alienation. Rigid control of freedom of speech and expression has not been able to suppress the growing cry for a human face to socialism.

(5) We continue to witness the agonizing protest of youth, who in many countries make up the majority of the population. They have played a crucial role in challenging racial and social injustice and demonic structures in education, work, and human relations — sometimes at the cost of brutal suppression. Youth have also expressed the spiritual hunger of our time. To be sure, many have sought mystical experience through drugs and Eastern religious practices, but many others are earnestly seeking in Christian faith and worship the spiritual resources to inspire and undergird their struggle for social justice. Contemplation and struggle are seen in a dynamic, prophetic relationship. Others attempt to overcome the anonymity and privatization of society by assembling in small, intense groups, some of them charismatic. The re-emergence of faiths other than the Christian faith and the search for world community in justice and peace with Christians are yet other signs of the times.

(6) The condition of the churches is itself a sign of the times. No longer are they a dominant and dominating force in society. The Constantinian era is over. Everywhere the church is or is becoming a minority, scattered in a society which ignores it or is hostile to it. Theological and ecclesiastical structures of thought and life, which have so often reflected and strengthened oppressive and unjust states, are now discredited. The churches are being forced to discover their role as the Body of Christ, the Servant of the Lord, what the Third Assembly of the

WCC called a "pilgrim church which goes forth boldly as Abraham did into the unknown future, not afraid to leave behind the securities of its conventional structures, glad to dwell in the tent of perpetual adaptation, looking to the city whose builder and maker is God."

How do these signs of the times affect our work of evangelization today? It cannot be taken for granted, of course, that the churches recognize or even try to understand the signs of the times. Jesus himself warned the religious leaders: "When you see a cloud looming up in the west you say at once that rain is coming, and so it does. And when the wind is from the south you say it will be hot, and it is. Hypocrites! You know how to interpret the face of the earth and the sky. How is it you do not know how to interpret these times?" (Luke 12:54-56). It is possible to be sensitive to the natural, traditional phenomena around us and yet insensitive to new and challenging issues of life-and-death significance for us. Jesus was himself the sign which illuminated all the signs of the times; yet people did not recognize him. We are less excusable, because we live in the reality of the finished work of Christ in his death and resurrection and in the dispensation of the Holy Spirit who enables us to discern and to act.

It is my conviction that these signs of the times, among others, constitute a genuine *praeparatio evangelica*. They demonstrate how human beings are on the one hand assuming responsibility for their existence as made in the image of God — even if they do not know or acknowledge him — and, on the other hand, are increasingly realizing that they cannot achieve an authentic existence in justice and peace on their own. Even some Marxists have spoken of the need for a transcendent humanism. It is, of course, true that this recognition is not universal. There may even be a majority of persons who are indifferent or reduced to nervous helplessness. But the hopeful sign is that even among these people there is an awakening consciousness of the human lot. This is, therefore, no time for the churches to relapse into fear and despair. Such pessimism is a denial of faith in our risen Lord and a misreading of the signs of the times.

But having said this, we must go on to insist that a relevant evangelism will depend on a radical change of attitude, thinking, speaking, and living in and among the churches. What then should be the form in which the evangelizing church exists today? We have been learning in the ecumenical movement that the only way forward is the way of dialogue with the modern world. Dialogue is not an intellectual exercise, not a programme or a fashion. It is not a means of discovering how others think and speak so that we can adapt our ready-made, traditional dogmatic answers. Dialogue is a form of existence, the form of the incarnate Lord as a servant living among human beings, open and vulnerable to them. It is the way of the cross. Or as Paul put it in his letter to the Philippians, it means to know Christ and commit ourselves to him "in the power of his resurrection and the fellowship of his sufferings" (3:10).

Jesus' ministry was one of dialogue with the poor and needy, the rich and the powerful, the sick and those who thought they were well, the religiously upright and the outcasts. It was in the dialogue of word and act, of debate and healing, that the good news was proclaimed. And the supreme proclamation was his solidarity, his life-giving dialogue with humanity on the cross when he cried: "My God, my God, why hast thou forsaken me?" The authenticity of our evangelization will depend on our willingness to assume this faithful risk of suffering love with human beings today.

Such a costly dialogue also demands taking others with radical seriousness in their particularities, their identities, their proper otherness. The gospels do not give us a dogmatic presentation of God's revelation in Christ, but tell a series of very diverse stories of Christ's concrete encounters with different human beings and groups.

As the Jewish philosopher Spinoza wrote: "The more we know things in their particularity, the more we know God." This means today that we must learn to respect people in their cultural and religious settings. Pluralism of life and response is not a danger to the uniqueness of the gospel. Rather it makes possible the expression of what both Paul and Peter described as the many-sided grace or wisdom of God. It affirms the true universality of the gospel as it finds its form in the soil of different cultures. The gospel by its very character challenges all peoples in their cultures, and yet it is their cultures which shape the human voice which must answer the voice of Christ. No true evangelization will result in copying foreign ways of accepting Christ.

This has two consequences for the evangelizing church. First, evangelization is not a strategy which can be worked out by the World Council of Churches, or by a synod of bishops, or by a world fellowship of evangelicals. It takes place in a given place and with particular persons or groups. Therefore, the base of evangelization is the local church, the whole people of God in the community as they worship, live, and work among people. What matters here is that there be a dialogue between local churches in mutual respect and correction, in a collegiality of sharing and being enriched by "the grace of God in its varied forms" (1 Pet. 4:10).

Secondly, evangelization which occurs in a given place and among people in their particularities must take into consideration the whole of the existence of the persons and groups. Word and act, proclamation and service, theology and praxis, contemplation and struggle, patient hope and urgent engagement are inextricably bound together as the proper rhythm of evangelization.

The challenge facing the churches is not whether the modern world is concerned or unconcerned about their evangelistic message, but rather whether the churches are so renewed in their life and thought that they become a living witness to the integrity of the gospel. The evangelizing churches need to receive the good news themselves and to let the Holy Spirit remake their life when and how he wills.

# 6. Working together for justice

*Our daily bread*

The profound concern of the churches for the plight of the vast millions of hungry poor who constitute the majority of the world's population is no new thing. Christianity has made the Hebrew prophetic cry for justice its own. Its very name derives from the one who came proclaiming the kingdom of God and his justice. He expressed this message in concrete words and acts on behalf of the hungry, the thirsty, the naked, the oppressed, and the marginalized, and he encouraged his followers to continue his attitude and actions: "As you do it to the least of these my brethren, you have done it to me" (Matt. 25: 40).

For nearly two thousand years Christians have sought to serve all those who are in distress of any kind. To help them to have a more humane existence, Christians have set up hospitals, schools, and agricultural projects, and have taught skills of various kinds. In fact, many of the foundations of the economic and social affluence of the rich countries today were laid by the intrepid and sacrificial efforts of Christian societies, monks, and orders. In the past two centuries of Western colonial and economic exploitation of underdeveloped countries, it has been the churches which have in large measure attempted to attend to the needs of the poor and oppressed, particularly through the work of mission and agencies of social service.

It is not surprising, then, that since its formation in 1948 the World Council of Churches has been engaged in activities of aid on a large scale and also in studies of the causes of poverty and injustice. Among its many statements on the problem of hunger in the world is this declaration from the Uppsala assembly in 1968:

New advances in agriculture hold the promise of freedom from hunger. But today world hunger must be a fundamental concern. The churches must insist that food is a resource which belongs to God and that all forces be mobilized to ensure that the earth produce adequate food for all. Agricultural policies should give primary emphasis to the alleviation of hunger.

Our experience since then has taught us that this matter needs to be approached at a deeper and more fundamental level. Development efforts so far have been powerless to redress the gap between the rich and the poor between and within nations. On the contrary, the gap grows wider every year. The world food crisis is only one tragic consequence of the widening gap. Several years of involvement in development aid have convinced us that a purely economic growth concept working automatically for development should be replaced by a process aimed at economic and social justice, self-reliance, and people's participation in establishing goals and priorities and making decisions regarding economic growth as a means to the end of a globally just society.

With such a vision of development we approach the present world food crisis. Through the centuries millions of people have suffered from hunger and poverty. The difference between previous times and the present is our full awareness today of the immensity of the problems facing the world's poor peoples. In their turn, the oppressed and the poor are no longer accepting their lot passively. They are rapidly becoming conscious that humanity has the means of enabling people to free themselves from want and fear and of creating a responsible society. The prevalent world monetary crisis, galloping inflation, oil and other commodity price increases, and above all the continual arms race have opened the eyes of the rich nations to the extreme precariousness of the present world economic and political systems. Furthermore, we know that this situation has been aggravated by short-sighted policies motivated by narrow provincial interests, administrative ineptitude everywhere, and a demonic attachment to the profit motive — whether through private, mixed, or state capitalism — which has benefited the already well-off in the developed and developing nations. Any development strategy which leaves the existing world economic and political structures essentially unchanged is doomed to failure, with unimaginable consequences for the human family.

There is no short-cut to meeting the permanent crisis of our irresponsible world society. We must also recognize the inadequacy, self-deception, and demagoguery in some of the long-term measures which have been proposed. For example, some have argued that all we really need is population control, which will make development aid and the transfer of grain to the needy more effective. Experience, however, has shown that it is precisely social and economic development which reduces income inequality, and this is a precondition for a decrease in the rate of population growth. Moreover, where there is a determined effort to promote participatory self-reliance and an economic policy aimed at social justice, as in China, the world's most populous nation, the problem of hunger can be substantially tackled.

Others have said that oil-rich countries should invest in the developing countries and therefore provide the necessary finance for purchasing food stocks from the developed countries. In fact, however, the present world monetary and economic system encourages the oil-producing countries, especially those which are underpopulated and underdeveloped, to protect themselves by investing in the rich countries in a manner which will enable them to survive when they can no longer rely on oil, their only economic resource. This in turn provides fresh capital for the rich countries, which are enabled to meet their own balance of payments problem, and perpetuates their capacity to sequester scarce food stocks for themselves.

There is also a tendency for the countries which have a grain monopoly to produce proposals for dealing with the food crisis which leave farmers' profits untouched — in other words, maintaining the prevailing economic system. But the farming policies of such nations are heavily protected, and their artificially dominating while fluctuating currencies always put the poor nations at a considerable disadvantage.

As a person from the Caribbean, recognizing that we in the islands are victims of international injustice, I must confess that our own governments and rich and powerful groups in our countries share responsibility for the present crisis. Within our

countries we have done little to reduce the gap between the rich
and the poor. We have neglected the poorest sectors of our
society. We have been aping development models of the rich
nations which are irrelevant to our own social, economic, and
cultural realities. We have worked in collusion with foreign
interests to exploit the poor masses, and in so doing have
adopted colonial or neo-colonial patterns of behaviour.
Without adopting radical measures to change the structures in
our society and adopting authentic goals and processes of
development, we do not earn the right to criticize the rich and
powerful elsewhere. We lack the moral credibility to propose
and effect changes in the global order.

Despite what we said about the churches' involvement in
relief of distressed peoples, the churches themselves do not have
a particularly good record seen from this angle. Christian individuals and groups have alleviated much human suffering and
need, but the churches are all too often accomplices in the
unjust structures of society. Often themselves conspicuously
wealthy, they have pursued prestige and position in society.
They have been devoted to acts of charity while being attached
to the existing economic and political systems. They have failed
to help Christians place the accent on being rather than having.
All this adds up to a heretical maintenance of the *status quo*.
Too often we as churches have indulged in exhorting the world
without rigorously examining ourselves and our practices. We
have been content to make pious appeals for solidarity and
generosity without facing their implications for a profound
transformation of the structures of our life as well as that of
society. As the apostle Peter wrote: "The time has come for
judgment to begin with the household of God."

The churches must reconsider their task in the light, not just
of the present crisis, but of the total ineffectiveness of our actual
economic and political structures. The present situation
requires a multi-faceted approach to achieve equitable financial
and trade practices, land reform, maximum participation of the
people in the development process, creating conditions and
greater facilities for the peasants (those most affected by the
crisis and the most neglected in our societies) to be the major
producers of food and other basic necessities.

While recognizing the limitations of the churches in facing these gigantic problems, we can discern the following immediate tasks of Christians and churches in both the developed and underdeveloped countries:

(1) Awakening the conscience of our people through preaching, teaching, and example, and thereby working for the mobilization of political will toward radical changes in the present international economic order. This includes taking steps to conscientize the rich everywhere to the need for a healthy reduction of their uncontrolled and suicidal consumer patterns and styles of life.

(2) Giving special attention to the needs of the poorest of the poor, especially in the Third World, and to improving the lot of rural peasants. To provide credit facilities for poor peasants, the World Council of Churches has taken a modest step in launching an Ecumenical Development Cooperative Society.

(3) Cooperating with people of all faiths and ideologies and with all movements struggling for justice, self-reliance, and the participation of all in decision-making toward economic growth for a shared life in community.

(4) Utilizing unused church lands, investments, and other resources for agricultural development in rural areas on a cooperative basis, and for promoting community health care, education, and social development wherever possible.

We Christians pray: "Give us this day our daily bread." But we know that the context of this prayer is the petition that God's kingdom of justice will come and that his will for a common life of solidarity and sharing on this earth will be done. It is also a prayer for forgiveness of our sins, our individual and collective greed and self-interest, and for being delivered from the evil which thwarts God's will for humanity.

The challenge with which the hungry millions confront the churches who make the Lord's Prayer their own is a call to move their concern beyond charity to a difficult engagement with daunting problems. But none of us who pray for our daily bread have the luxury of disregarding that call.

## Peace: the fruit of justice

The prophet speaks of the day when "the Spirit is poured upon us from on high, and the wilderness becomes a fruitful field, and the fruitful field is deemed a forest. Then justice will dwell in the wilderness, and righteousness abide in the fruitful field. And the fruit of righteousness will be peace, and the result of righteousness, undisturbed security for ever" (Isa. 32:15-17).

The key words in this prophetic vision of a new world are righteousness, justice, peace, and undisturbed security. In their Hebrew forms, these familiar words are packed with meaning. Righteousness, *tsedeq*, comes from a Semitic root which means to be straight, firm, steel-like, as opposed to evil, *rasha*, to be loose or slack, to ignore or forget. To be just is to be straight, right, attentive, acting according to one's inner being, having integrity of character. For example, the Arabic equivalent of *tsedeq* is used to describe a date which is fully mature, which tastes as it ought to taste. This is precisely what God has been. He is revealed as utterly true and utterly faithful because he promises good to the covenant people. God has been concerned about their highest interests, concerned that the divine image in them should be realized. Thus he demands that the people should be righteous, that they have integrity of being before God and in their dealing with each other as sharing a common humanity. As John Skinner says, for the prophets righteousness "includes a large-hearted construction of the claims of humanity; it is...the humanitarian virtue *par excellence.*" To be righteous is to be fully human, firm, strong, integrated into God's purpose of good for others and for the whole of creation.

Justice, *mishpat*, has the sense of behaving according to God's declared righteous will, practicing fair dealing. Justice is the day-to-day conduct of one who is righteous, righteousness in action.

Peace, *shalom*, means entirety, totality, wholeness. It is the undisturbed freedom of life and movement, the unchecked growth and expansion of the self. *Shalom* prevails in those who are united in acting together for the common good; it represents the Hebrew conception of history as harmonious community. Far more than the mere absence of conflict and war, it indicates the state in which all human beings and all things are able to be and fulfil themselves unchecked and undisturbed.

Security, *betach*, means being able to trust one another, to abandon oneself to mutual confidence. Related to it in the text is the word quietness, *shaqet*, which again means undisturbed, unchecked.

What the prophet is saying is that in the chaos of injustice, conflict, and war, God pours out his live-giving and power-enabling Spirit, as he did at creation. There at the beginning God created order in the chaos, form and substance in the void, through the Spirit. Above all God created man and woman in the divine image to deal with creation in a spirit of good and to replenish the earth for good. Now there is chaos again because of the evil which humanity has brought on the earth. Things have become slack and loose. There is no firmness, no sense of wholeness, no trust or security among people. Creation itself is out of joint, despoiled, and in danger of being destroyed. In this situation God sends the Spirit to bring righteousness, justice, peace, and undisturbed security among men and women and in creation itself. All of this is God's work, not ours. We can never achieve justice and peace ourselves. We can only receive them from God as a gift according to his design.

But what is God's gift is also our work as those made in the image of God. The prophet says at the beginning of this chapter 32:

> Behold, a king shall reign in righteousness, and his rulers rule with justice, and a man shall be a refuge from the wind and a shelter from the tempest, like streams of water in a dry ground, like the shade of a great rock in a weary land (Isa. 32:1-2).

What is God's gift is humanity's task. The king and the rulers in this passage are representatives of what everyone should be — righteous and just, persons of integrity who deal rightly with others according to God's will and action.

The prophet provides a beautiful image of what this means. In the storms which arise in the desert, it is good to have a rock to provide refuge from the wind and shelter from the storm. Moreover, the rock prevents the ground from becoming dried out and so arrests the drift of the soil into the desert. A righteous, just person is one of rocklike character, who prevents the drift into chaos and disaster, provides shelter, and becomes a source of growth for others. Justice is related to fruitful soil and the right use of creation. A just society depends on just persons of rocklike integrity.

In discussing war and peace, militarism, the arms race and disarmament, we often spend a great deal of energy analyzing and making proposals about what needs to be done. We have not sufficiently emphasized the absolute importance of personal involvement and responsibility. Overwhelmed by systems, structures, powers, and the frightening dimensions of the conflicts in our world, we are inclined to lose a sense of our personal and corporate responsibility. This is what the prophet calls us back to. God's design and promise demand that we are each and all engaged in his work of justice and peace. At a 1978 special session of the UN General Assembly on Disarmament, I said:

> Disarmament is not the affair of statesmen and experts only, but of every man and woman of every nation. We are dealing here with the issues of life and death for humankind. They are not technical, but human and therefore political issues. This means that every effort must be made to dispel the ignorance, complacency, and fear which prevail.... The churches have a very distinctive role to play because they have the criterion of faith in the God of hope, whose purpose is that all should be responsible for each other in justice and peace. Therefore they will continue to arouse the conscience of people and encourage them to demonstrate by attitude, word, and act that peace and justice are not ideals to be cherished but realities to be achieved. The arms race is the decision and creation of human beings. Disarmament must also be willed and won by human beings.

What are the human causes and cure of injustice and conflicts? This is precisely what the prophet seeks to face in this chapter. He says that when each person practices justice and is rocklike in integrity of character:

> Then the eyes of those who see will not be closed, and the ears of those who hear will listen. The anxious heart will understand and know, and the tongue of the stammerers will speak readily and distinctly (Isa. 32:3-4).

What the prophet is saying is that in the struggle for justice and peace, one of the big stumbling blocks is the refusal of people to see the issues and hear about the realities around them. He puts it more precisely when he appeals to the women as representative of this tragic human habit:

> Rise up, you women who are at ease, hear my voice; you complacent young women, give ear to my speech. In little more than a year you will shudder, you complacent women; for the vintage will fail, the fruit harvest will not come. Tremble, you women who are at ease, shudder, you complacent ones; strip, and make yourselves bare, and gird sackcloth upon your loins (Isa. 32:9-11).

What the prophet is describing so graphically has been the experience of our lifetime. In spite of World War I and the depression of the early 1930s, the Western world remained at ease and complacent, seeing and yet refusing to see, hearing and yet refusing to listen. The result was World War II and the holocaust. The biggest danger of today's consumer societies is that we accept things as they are, refusing to probe deeper and work for change. This is particularly the case at present with regard to the arms race. The tendency is to feel that nothing can be done about it, and all we can do is to wait for the holocaust which will engulf us all. In the meantime, we will take our ease and be complacent, though deep down there is a sense of fatalism, fear, and despair. In other societies, tyrants and militarists make sure that people neither see nor hear and are left with their anxious hearts and stammering tongues, unable to understand and know and speak up.

The challenge to us who are bearers of justice and peace is to seek the power of the Spirit to enable people to see, speak, and listen in love. For it is precisely this which marks us out as human beings made in the image of God. When people cannot or will not speak or listen, they lose their humanity — and that is the absence of justice and peace and security. As Rosenstock-Huessy taught us, "God is the power who makes us speak." We experience God and therefore come into the sphere of justice and peace when we can reach beyond ourselves in solidarity with others, rather than sit at ease and in complacency, and when we can speak the word which needs to be said and listen to what is being spoken to us. It is in such speaking and listening that we can move into God's future of justice and peace.

This can be perceived in the current talk of national security. It has been exalted into a dogma which is employed to justify arms build-ups, military takeovers, the suppression of civilian political institutions and the violation of human rights. In the defense of "law and order" sinister instruments of torture, police and prison hardware, and sophisticated means of intelligence-gathering have been produced. Moreover, in the name of national security, the mass media and educational institutions are frequently misused to foster a psychosis of fear and mistrust and to prevent any other way of looking at the resolution of conflicts than in military terms. Indeed, national security becomes a means of muzzling and blinding people.

The prophet goes on to say that the person who becomes righteous and just and who is enabled to see, speak, and listen displays a clear-eyed discernment of the real nature of people and things. Once more he puts the issue very realistically:

> The fool will no more be called noble, nor the knave said to be honourable. For the fool speaks folly, and his mind plots iniquity; to practice ungodliness, to utter error concerning the Lord. He starves the hungry of food, and refuses drink to the thirsty. The knaveries of the knave are evil; he devises wicked plans to ruin the poor with lying words, and deny justice to the needy. But the person who is noble devises noble things, and by noble things stands firm (Isa. 32:5-8).

One of the most astonishing things about our unstable and unjust world is how realities are covered up and false estimates and values are made about them. The powerful cover up their folly and villainy by high-sounding names and postures. Things are not called by their proper names. For example, the ideologies of capitalism and Communism are used as slogans to hide various forms of national self-interest. Whenever and wherever people revolt against oppression — racial, economic, political — the slogans are immediately invoked. The Americans and Westerners accuse them of being Communists — and that becomes an excuse for supporting tyrants and knaves. The Russians and socialist states call them running dogs of capitalist imperialism — and so justify their brutal suppression of peoples or imprisonment of persons.

Furthermore, there is the conventional wisdom of the various ideologies, which leave no room for examination or change. A glaring example is South Africa, which claims to defend Christian values and civilization and the sacred system of free enterprise by practicing apartheid and ruthlessly oppressing the black people. Western investments and arms sales help to maintain the racist system, and the rationale which is given is that these steps defend capitalist free enterprise against the encroachment of Communist collectivism.

In this situation words and values lose their meaning and people are so confused that they are no longer able to discern the issues. The result is injustice, armed conflict, and senseless violence.

The prophet is calling on us to have the moral insight and courage to expose this folly and villainy which "ruin the poor with lies and deny justice to the needy." To be just and to seek peace is to be noble — open-hearted, open-handed, magnanimous, firm, having integrity, calling things by their proper names, treating human beings humanly, not ignoring or separating ourselves from them.

Victor Hugo wrote: "There are no weeds in society, only bad cultivators." The vision of a just society is the challenge to be just persons, to let ourselves be guided and governed, enlivened and empowered by the Spirit of God. Jesus, the embodiment of justice and peace, told us: "Blessed are the peacemakers, for they will be called the children of God." In seeking to make peace we are placing ourselves in the way of God's will and so are fulfilling God's design that we become truly human and just and be God's children by sharing this life with our brothers and sisters. For as the apostle Paul says in Romans 8:19: "The whole creation waits with eager longing for the revealing of the children of God."

Centuries old, the words of Isaiah 32 offer an up-to-date guide in talking about peace, harmonious community, and security as the achievement of righteousness and justice. "Happy are you who sow beside *all* waters, who let the feet of the ox and the ass range free" (Isa. 32:20) was paraphrased by a nineteenth-century commentator: "Happy are they who go steadily on, doing the work committed to them by God, alike in storm and in sunshine, confiding in the righteousness of God." That is the way of justice and peace.

*Christian communities and human rights*

The voice of the church is one of many which have been heard on the subject of human rights over the past several years. To a certain extent, "human rights" has become a slogan, an in-phrase. Some of those speaking the loudest have used human rights as a propaganda tool to attack each other across the ideological and political barriers that divide our world, all but forgetting the millions of people who in fact suffer from the deprivation of those rights — people who are hurt and angry but cannot express themselves with the sophistication and disinterestedness in which others have indulged during these years. With all the time and energy the churches have spent discussing human rights, our understanding has grown. In the hope of increasing this clarity, let me make a few brief comments on human rights in an ecumenical perspective.

In the first place we have not yet faced all the implications of the indivisibility of civil and political rights *and* economic, social, and cultural rights. In the aftermath of World War II the predominant theme was civil and political rights, because the totalitarian regimes had flouted those rights so flagrantly. In the following years when the covenants implementing the United Nations Declaration of Human Rights were being discussed, these were divided into two separate documents — civil and political rights on the one hand and social, economic, and cultural rights on the other. But Christians cannot accept this separation along the lines of the ideological divisions in the world. Political and civil rights are undergirded by economic, social, and cultural rights, and vice versa. Human rights are as indivisible as the gospel itself. In the East-West and North-South conflicts of our time, however, there is a tendency for one party to use one set of human rights to attack the other party.

For example, we who are not Irish try to grasp the agony surrounding the churches and human rights in Northern Ireland. Most of us have a vague impression that the issues are mainly civil and political with a strong dash of religious antagonism thrown in. But in fact the history of Ireland since the Reformation, and certainly since Cromwellian times, has been one of blatant economic, social, and cultural exploitation and violation. Different confessions have been ranged on various sides of this exploitation and violation and in varying proportions as time has gone on. It is therefore no surprise that churches in Ireland find it so difficult to understand what is happening in southern Africa and the extent to which our countries are involved in maintaining a racist system where civil and political rights are denied, precisely because of economic, social, and cultural oppression maintained through investments, bank loans, sale of arms, and military alliances. When people do not face the totality of human rights in their own country they can hardly appreciate it in others. And what is true of Ireland is equally the case in all countries today.

Second, we have not perceived sufficiently the global dimensions of human rights. We have tended to assume that the arena in which human rights are to be exercised and promoted is our own community or nation or group of nations. But in the global village, we are politically and economically bound together. The violation of individual or social rights in one part of the world is often stimulated and maintained by other parts of the world. There is solidarity in sin just as there ought to be solidarity through grace in the struggle for implementing human rights. A massive and urgent task before the churches is to enable people to relate their local struggles to the global struggle. Allied to this is the fact that we cannot speak about human rights without speaking of the effects of transnational corporations, militarism and the arms race, racism, sexism, and the search for a new international economic order. Intellectually, of course, we prefer to have terms neatly defined, so that we can more easily deal with the reality described. But life is not like that. Human rights are concerned with right relations in all their aspects and about *the right* — justice, that which is proper and necessary to a full human existence.

A third remark is in order here. Sooner or later in discussing human rights someone is bound to observe that, while we must all work for right or justice in the world, we are also persons with responsibilities, obligations, and duties. Whenever I am tempted to speak in this fashion, I have to remind myself that over half of the population of this planet cannot freely exercise responsibilities, obligations, and duties. Indeed, duties are oppressively inflicted upon them, not for their benefit, but for the benefit of others — including ourselves as privileged persons and peoples. *We* assume our rights and howl when they are denied. *They* have few or no rights as human beings.

It is therefore significant that while the Bible does not speak in general terms of human rights, it does speak of establishing, affirming, and recognizing the right of the poor, the widow, the orphan, the alien. There is a deep insight here which we should not lose among our theological and linguistic niceties. The poor and the oppressed hold up mirrors to our humanity. They show us how distorted and truncated our own humanity is when our fellow human beings are deprived of their humanity. When we recognize our solidarity with the poor and the oppressed, when they are enabled to liberate themselves from their oppressors, it is not only they but also their oppressors who are liberated. Human rights is a striking expression to bring strongly before us the cries of more than half of the human race, cries which should become our cries for a more human existence.

These points lead us to some theological reflections on human rights. Such theological reflection, however, can have integrity only to the extent that it grows out of Christian communities which seek to live in penitent renewal through word and sacrament.

My first point is that humanity is made in the image of God and remade in Christ. The Jewish rabbis interpreted the creation of humanity in this way: "Therefore, everyone is bound to say: 'On account of me, the world was created.' That means: 'Everyone is to feel himself/herself individually responsible, as though the whole human race depend on his or her conduct.'" The Jewish Mishna included an admonition that every witness in a murder case must say the following: "For this reason a single man only was created: to teach you that if one destroys a single person, the Scripture imputes it to him as though he has destroyed the whole world." From this one rabbi enunciated the principle that "the image of God must be reverenced in our common humanity." This unity of humankind permits — indeed, enjoins — solidarity with all human beings, whatever their race, nationality, class, or religion. We have a common ground of being. Just as we are made for conversation with God, we are by that very fact made for conversation with each other. The image of God is therefore a call to the true democratization of all society, in which human beings claim and exercise their rights in response to God's purpose and in mutual responsibility.

Secondly, we are created as persons in relation, different and yet alike, participating in the same task as representatives of the Creator over creation. Being in a complementary relationship with each other, we must affirm and assert the other and be willing to share in what God has given us. This is immensely important in our shrinking world. We talk mainly about the conflicts of that closeness, but fail to appreciate sufficiently the immense wealth of opportunities for sharing our different cultures, sharing in our otherness as human beings. The essence of the unity of the church about which the ecumenical movement speaks so often is the communion among people, which Jesus' prayer in John 17 compares to sharing in the divine Godhead. Paul makes the point with equal strength in 1 Corinthians 12, with his image of the body: the eye cannot say to the mouth, "I have no need of you; I am the whole body." Everyone has an integrity, an identity of his or her own, without which the whole body is broken and cannot function. This is a vital issue for us when we speak about human rights in terms of our being in the image of God. And when we speak about participation, it is a recognition of the integrity of the gifts of the other and at the same time of the fact that we cannot function without all sharing with each other.

A third theological reflection on human rights is the understanding that humanity, male and female, is called to be masters of creation, but masters of creation to replenish the earth for the good of all. God gives his blessing to us, empowers us, so that we may in turn empower each other and use our power over nature for the well-being of all and the fulfilment of creation. It is in that sense that we speak about the economic and social rights, the right to live, the right to work, and so on. This whole aspect of anthropology needs to be developed more than we have done so far. We have spoken too superficially about the image of God.

A fourth area for theological reflection on human rights is the idea of covenant. Protestants — particularly those of the Reformed tradition — use this term quite a bit when discussing human rights. Sometimes the theological idea is linked with Thomas Hobbes's notion of a social contract. The danger here is that of making the connection exclusively with the old covenant and neglecting the new covenant. The heart of the new covenant is *kenosis*, the self-emptying of God which leads to the cross. It is in Philippians 2 that Paul develops this idea, and it is precisely there that he is talking about our respect for each other and our willingness to put the interests of others above our own. Christ, who had all power and privilege, was willing to empty himself. This is the centre of any covenant relationship: the willingness to forgo what is rightfully ours for the sake of others. This aspect of covenant theology needs further working out.

Finally, what can we say about the kinds of Christian communities who will be involved in the issue of human rights?

The first remark is a confession: as the inheritors of the Christian tradition we have an appalling history to live down. Since Christianity became an established religion under the Emperor Constantine, the violation of human rights has been very much the work of the churches. Inquisitions and ordeals and heresy trials provided models for torture and the denial of human rights. So when we talk about this matter today, we do so in an attitude of penitence and humility and a willingness to ask ourselves how much those attitudes are still with us.

The second comment is that the churches have played an active role in promoting human rights. The story of the writing of the Universal Declaration of Human Rights is a story of the active involvement of church people, both clergy and laity. Moreover, the Roman Catholic Church and the World Council of Churches have in the past fifteen years been doing a considerable amount of work in relation to human rights. In a joint appeal which Cardinal Roy, then president of the Pontifical Commission of Justice and Peace, and I wrote some years ago to commemorate the twenty-fifth anniversary of the Universal Declaration of Human Rights, we summarized some of the insights which have emerged as churches worked together for human rights. We appealed to local churches and particularly Christian leaders and educators to initiate or intensify programmes to instruct and sensitize Christians about human rights and corresponding duties, so that all people, regardless of race, religion, class, or nationality, might be aware of the qualities of human life to which they are entitled. Together we must promote and defend human rights in our own respective societies and in solidarity with all those who struggle for freedom and justice. We must redouble our efforts to remove the root causes of human suffering.

This is a call to pastoral action. It requires the mobilization of all men and women in local and national churches with experience in the field of human rights. Among the elements in such a strategy are practical catechetical education, preaching on the biblical motivation for human rights, informed reflection on the changing social and economic situation in the world and on the need to protect the personal rights of the poor and despised — all in order to prepare congregations and individuals for difficult and costly decisions in the area of human rights.

The words of Paul in Romans 8 challenge and sustain a Christian commitment to human rights. When we have been enabled to find our way as human beings through God's light on us, when we have learned to live by his Spirit and to call him "Abba, Father," when we have reached that point of security, we are immediately called to suffer with Christ. Such suffering is not something abstract; it has to do with the travailing creation waiting for the revelation of the children of God, waiting for us.

But who are we? We do not know how to cope. We do not know how to speak. We do not even know how to pray. But God's Spirit comes to our aid, and because he does, God works the purpose of his creation. What is most incredible is the assurance that neither life nor death, nor principalities nor powers, nor things present nor things to come nor any created thing can separate us from God's love — that love which unites the separated, breaks down the apartheids of our world, unites us to ourselves, to one another, and to the Godhead.

## Religious liberty in an ecumenical perspective

We stressed in the preceding section that human rights must be understood as indivisible — that the separation of civil and political rights from social, economic, and cultural ones is unacceptable on the basis of a Christian understanding of history and the gospel. Without in any way contradicting this insight, let us now focus briefly on a particular human right with which the churches have been intimately concerned — religious liberty.

Freedom of religion was on the agenda at the first assembly of the World Council of Churches in 1948; and although our understanding of it has evolved since then, the Amsterdam Declaration on Religious Liberty remains substantially valid as a statement of the basis of the concern of the ecumenical movement in the area:

> An essential element in a good international order is freedom of religion.... Christians, therefore, view the question of religious freedom as an international problem. They are concerned that religious freedom be everywhere secured. In pleading for this freedom, they do not ask for any privilege to be granted to Christians that is denied to others. While the liberty with which Christ has set men free can neither be given nor destroyed by any government, Christians, because of that inner freedom, are both jealous of its outward expression and solicitous that all men should have freedom in religious life. The nature and destiny of man by virtue of his creation, redemption and calling, and man's activities in family, state and culture establish limits beyond which the government cannot with impunity go. The rights which Christian discipleship demands are such as are good for all men, and no nation has ever suffered by reason of granting such liberties.

In fact, ecumenical thinking and engagement in the field of religious liberty antedates 1948. At the 1945 San Francisco conference which gave birth to the United Nations a representative of the churches acted as spokesman for numerous nongovernmental organizations in seeking provision for a commission on human rights in the UN charter. He was Dr. O. Frederick Nolde, who became the following year the first director of the Commission of the Churches on International Affairs (CCIA), a body established jointly by the World Council of Churches in Process of Formation and the International Missionary Council. Nolde participated alongside governmental representatives in drafting the Universal Declaration of Human Rights, serving specially as consultant on religious liberty and freedom of conscience. In the years following the adoption of the Universal Declaration, the CCIA was constantly present to advise, to lobby, and push the UN through the elaboration of the international covenants on human rights.

Just as theology was long considered the queen of the sciences, religious liberty was in the early years of the WCC a sort of "prince of human rights." There were three reasons for this. First, ecumenical concern for human rights emerged from the missionary stream of our tradition, with its urgent concern to remove barriers to the propagation of the gospel. Thus, the freedom to "hold and change one's faith, to express it in worship and practice, to teach and persuade others, and to decide on the religious education of one's children" was of central importance. Second, much of our ecumenical action on human rights was focused on establishing international standards through the United Nations. It was natural to assume that our greatest expertise, and therefore our most important contribution, was in the field of religious liberty. Finally, many of us were steeped in a juridical, philosophical, and theological orientation which considered religious liberty the cornerstone of the entire edifice of human rights. One did not limit one's concern exclusively to religious freedom, but when one engaged in efforts to establish and protect other essential rights, it was *in order that* full religious liberty could exist.

On this third point we can see a subtle but important shift in orientation, beginning with a study on "Christian Witness, Proselytism and Religious Liberty in the Setting of the WCC," initiated in 1956 and given final form at the New Delhi Assembly in 1961. Part of the impetus for this study, which rejected the concept of "proselytism" in favour of the term "Christian witness," was a 1920 encyclical of the Ecumenical Patriarchate on the so-called "conversion" of Orthodox Christians to "Western Christianity." Thus its main thrust was on relations among the WCC member churches. It affirmed that "it is a purpose of the WCC to help several churches so to carry on their witness as to strengthen one another... [and not] to seek... institutional advantage at the cost of... disadvantage to another." In the light of important technological, sociological, and political developments, it called for a critical review of a seventeenth-century philosophy largely centred on religious liberty. Finally, it made a fundamental point which was to shape much of our future world. The Assembly stated firmly that "the conscience of persons whose religious faith and convictions differ from our own must be recognized and respected." Though maintained as a central concern, religious liberty was placed in a new context.

Since then the WCC has become deeply engaged in a number of important areas: decolonization, self-determination of peoples, the struggle against racism, economic development, dialogue with people of other faiths and ideologies, equality of women and men, to mention only a few. Reflecting on that experience, and taking particularly into account the views of the member churches in Africa, Asia, and Latin America, a consultation on "Human Rights and Christian Responsibility" held at St Pölten, Austria, in 1974 stated:

> The WCC has frequently declared that religious liberty *is* a basic human right. This right is required so that the full responsibilities of Christian faith may be undertaken. [It] is not a privilege or an exclusive freedom for the church. Human solidarity demands that we should be aware of the inter-relatedness of all rights including the rights of those of other faiths or no faiths.... The right to religious liberty exists in order to serve the community according to the demands of the Gospel.

Ecumenical thinking has challenged liberal philosophies of rights in another important way. In 1948 there was a very strong interest in the rights of the individual to exercise his or her religious freedom. This approach views corporate rights as derived from the rights of individual persons, in a sort of inverted pyramid in which the number of individuals whose rights are assured gradually increases, finally arriving at the rights of the group, the collective, the people, and the nation. The experience of the WCC over the years has shown that this philosophical concept is one-sided and misleading. We have come to recognize more clearly that the individual is inevitably linked to and part of a community. It is illusory to think that the right of a South African black to participate in decision-making in society can ever be secured so long as she is relegated by the apartheid system to a subhuman condition. It is inconceivable that the right of a peasant in the Sahel to adequate food, housing, and health care can ever be realized so long as the world economy is structured in a way that keeps his country in a state of penury.

Theologically, as well, we have been forced to challenge the liberal approach to individual rights. The Fifth Assembly of the WCC (Nairobi, 1975) had as its main theme "Jesus Christ Frees and Unites." It is implicit in that affirmation that Christ has freed us not to live in individual isolation, but to unite us in service to the poor, to the oppressed, to those who languish in prisons, to those who hunger and thirst for righteousness' sake.

In order to fulfil this command of the gospel we must become alert to that which foments poverty, captivity, and inequality, maintains the structures of injustice, and vitiates the legitimate rights of others.

This does not mean that the ecumenical movement has abandoned its concern for the individual or its efforts to protect his or her rights. Far from it. As the St Pölten consultation put it:

> Individual rights and collective rights are not in flat opposition. They are related. It should be the aim of the community to secure the welfare of all its members, the aim of the individual to serve the general good. In both instances rights involve responsibilities.

It is therefore important to challenge any society which, for the sake of what it calls national security or the common good, flagrantly denies the rights of individuals who, for the sake of the same common good, give voice to the violation of human rights, including religious liberty. Both individual *and* corporate rights must be respected.

Our concern for religious freedom has often been linked with what has sometimes been called the "what-is-wrong-elsewhere" approach. In the beginning, the WCC was composed largely of churches from the Western, industrialized part of the world, with its marked tendency to give priority attention to violations of others' rights, to restrictions on others' freedoms, and to neglect or take a less critical view of their own situation. Interwoven with this was the often tacit assumption that the ideological, cultural, and philosophical concepts of one's own society had universal validity, and formed the indispensable standard by which to judge the behaviour of other nations and cultures. Our statements and interventions on matters of religious freedom have not been immune from such tendencies.

The Nairobi Assembly spoke of the need "to become ever more active in identifying and rectifying violations of human rights in our own societies, and to enter into new forms of ecumenical solidarity with Christians elsewhere who are similarly engaged." This concept of ecumenical solidarity through new forms of relationships among the churches and with others has proved to be extremely important for our life together in today's world. It is not, however, a new idea to the ecumenical movement. The study on religious liberty considered by the New Delhi Assembly in 1961 included this statement:

That we in our churches respect the convictions of other churches whose conception and practice of church membership differs from our own and consider it our Christian duty to pray for one another and to help each other rise above our respective short-comings through frank theological interchange, experience or common worship and concrete acts of mutual service; and that we recognize it as our obligation when in exceptional cases private or public criticism of another church seems to be required of us, first to examine ourselves and always to speak the truth in love to the edification of the churches.

To speak the truth in love is never the easy way. To speak our truth to others elsewhere about their responsibility may be costly to a relationship we hold dear. But the truly costly discipleship about which Bonhoeffer spoke requires speaking the truth in love to ourselves, to our own churches, and to the authorities of our own nations.

The concern expressed in Amsterdam in 1948 about flagrant violations of human rights in many parts of the world, and its call for the churches to take a firm and vigorous stand against them has not waned in the decades since. If anything, it has become more acute, for the world situation itself has become more acute. As Nairobi said:

In our fallen world, there is no nation where human rights have been fully achieved. Because of discrepancies between what we profess and what we practise it is crucial for the churches to move from making *declarations* about human rights, to working for the full *implementation* of those rights.

The churches have not ceased to proclaim their right to religious freedom. But more significantly the churches in many parts of the world are no longer merely appealing to national authorities for religious tolerance, but are also exercising their freedom in Christ to stand up against those who show a patent disregard for humanity. They do not claim rights for themselves, but freedom and justice for all women and men in society. This exercise of freedom, this engagement for justice leads not infrequently today to the prison gate or directly to the cross. Public protests by Brazilian Catholic bishops against torture, political repression, and exploitation of the poor are met with beating, assassinations of priests and church workers, and all manner of threats against others. Christians in Argentina who seek to aid refugees from dictatorial regimes elsewhere in South America are kidnapped by hooded bands and caused to "disappear." A Christian lawyer in Indonesia who has the courage to defend political prisoners is himself imprisoned. South Korean Christians' quiet, nonviolent appeals for the restoration of democracy to their country lead to their being jailed. Other cases could be cited from around the world where Christians and others have suffered in various ways for their stands in favour of justice and human dignity in their own societies.

These are all concrete actions to match the words of the declaration of the Nairobi Assembly that religious liberty includes "the right and duty of religious bodies to criticize the ruling powers when necessary, on the basis of their religious convictions." In today's world it is this element in religious liberty which is most violently contested by state authorities and other power interests. And yet it belongs to the centre of our participation in God's kingdom and his justice that the crown rights of our Redeemer are claimed for every sphere of life. The liberty to believe, to worship, and to preach and teach carries the responsibility to make known in word and deed the fullness of the gospel. To do this is to follow in the footsteps of our Lord and to bear humbly and courageously the cross of opposition and persecution in the power of his resurrection.

*Racism in the 1960s*

No doubt the most visible programme of the World Council of Churches over the past several years has been its engagement in the worldwide struggle against racism. Our purpose here is not to discuss or defend specific actions or decisions taken to implement that commitment, but rather to set forth briefly how biblically based this concern has always been in the World Council of Churches and how it continues to be a top priority in the 1980s.

In fact, the foundation of this concern of the World Council of Churches can be traced to the very words of the Council's own basis:

> The World Council of Churches is a fellowship of churches which confess the Lord Jesus Christ as God and Saviour according to the Scriptures and therefore seek to fulfil together their common calling to the glory of the one God, Father, Son, and Holy Spirit.

To confess Jesus Christ is to acknowledge that he is Lord and
Saviour, Liberator of the whole human race and of the whole
creation. This was the first lesson that the early Christian
church had to learn, and it learned it in its first major crisis.
Should the gospel be proclaimed to the Gentiles and could they
be members of the same body of Christ as the Jews? When
Paul, a fervent Jew, was confronted with Christ and accepted
him as his Lord and Saviour, he realized that the inescapable
logic of his new-found faith was that it is for all. Writing to the
Galatians he reflects on the debate with the Jewish churches in
Jerusalem. He says clearly and unequivocally:

> For as many of you as were baptized into Christ have put on
> Christ. There is neither Jew nor Greek, there is neither slave nor
> free, there is neither male nor female; for you are all one in Christ
> Jesus (Gal. 3:27-28).

Paul goes on in this letter to insist that Gentiles do not have
to become Jews in order to be Christians. Becoming a Jew
meant being circumcized and observing certain traditional
practices. Paul declares: "In Christ Jesus neither circumcision
nor uncircumcision is of any avail, but faith working through
love" (Gal. 5:6). When Christ frees us as human beings, he liberates us to be our true selves, to have our own identity, whatever our race or sex, our tribe or nation, and whatever we are.
But our cultural, racial, and sexual identity, our liberation,
exists as a commitment to love; and this love is manifested in
our placing all we are and have at the disposal of others. As we
saw in chapter 2, the freedom to which we are called is not to be
used as an opportunity for the flesh (individual or group self-
assertion), but through love we are to be servants of one
another (Gal. 5:13).

Paul develops his understanding of the nature of the Christian community as the body of Christ. Each member of the
body has a different function and its own identity. To deny that
identity would be to deny the body itself. Moreover, these
varied members are indispensable for the functioning of the
body. They can only function in and for the body when they
are recognized as being and having an essential part in it. And
they can only maintain their functioning life when they are not
separated or do not separate themselves from the body (1 Cor.

12:12-27). Paul is unsparing in his criticism of those who separate themselves from others at the Lord's supper, consuming the bread and the wine, even to the point of drunkenness, while others are hungry. Such persons bring condemnation upon themselves, he says. They deny the very nature of the eucharist, in which we celebrate Christ's giving his body and blood for us. We partake of his body and blood so that we may offer our body and blood for others.

Paul, however, was haunted by the other fact — that Jews would not accept their place in the life of the body of Christ as a fulfilment of their calling (Romans 9-11). It was true that they were called as God's own people. But their calling was out of slavery and domination by Egypt. The God who liberated them from slavery did so in order to demonstrate his creative purpose that all made in his image should share a common life of good. The vocation of his liberated people, therefore, was to make this known to the world by their inner covenant life in justice, common trust, and peace. The whole thrust of the revelation in the Old Testament, culminating in the prophets, was that Israel was to be the servant, the slave, of God to fulfil his purpose of liberating all persons and peoples — not least the oppressors and imperialists — for true human life in community. Isaiah had a vision of this liberation of both the oppressed and the oppressors:

> In that day there will be a highway from Egypt to Assyria, and the Assyrian will come into Egypt, and the Egyptian into Assyria, and the Egyptians will worship with the Assyrians. In that day Israel will be the third with Egypt and Assyria, a blessing in the midst of the earth, whom the Lord of hosts has blessed, saying, "Blessed be Egypt my people, and Assyria the work of my hands, and Israel my heritage" (Isa. 19:23-25).

That vision later developed in terms of Israel, whether collectively or as a person acting on behalf of all, as the servant, the slave, so that true liberation and fullness of life might be received and shared by all (Isa. 42:1-9; 49:1-6; 50:4-9; 52:13-53:12).

In a divided world and in the midst of persons divided within themselves, Jesus comes, emptying himself of all the majesty and transcendent power of divine life, to be the servant, the slave, giving himself up to the very symbol of human and imperial oppression, the cross, so that all might be liberated. That is what his people, his body, the church, is called to be and to do in order to continue his ministry of liberation for a life of mutual trust and sharing by all (Phil. 2:1-11).

This is our confession of faith and our common calling. Therefore, when the World Council of Churches was formed in 1948, it was bound to say in its message to the churches:

> We have to learn afresh together to speak boldly in Christ's name both to those in power and to the people, to oppose terror, cruelty and race discrimination, to stand by the outcast, the prisoner and the refugee. We have to make of the Church in every place a voice for those who have no voice, and a home where every man will be at home.

It went on to declare:

> The Church as a worshipping body is the community of people who have found oneness in Jesus Christ. We strongly affirm our conviction that the Body of Christ cannot be divided by racial, class and other discriminations, and that any church or Christian group which upholds them in the name of Christ, is denying the very meaning of the Christian faith....
>
> If the Church can overcome the national and social barriers which now divide it, it can help society to overcome those barriers. This is especially clear in the case of racial distinction. It is here that the Church has failed most lamentably, where it has reflected and then by its example sanctified the racial prejudice that is rampant in the world. And yet it is here that today its guidance concerning what God wills for it is especially clear. It knows that it must call society away from prejudice based upon race or colour and from the practices of discrimination and segregation as denials of justice and human dignity, but it cannot say a convincing word to society unless it takes steps to eliminate these practices from the Christian community, because they contradict all that it believes about God's love for all His children.

From the outset, in other words, the World Council has recognized that racism symbolizes the denial of the biblical revelation and is the most evident manifestation of the disunity of the church and the disunity of humankind. Hence, if the Council is to be true to its purpose of working with and for the member churches for the unity of the body of Christ and thus for the unity of all persons and peoples made in the image of God, it was bound and is bound to give a high priority to the combat against racism.

Particular impetus for these commitments at Amsterdam came from an outstanding ecumenical statesman, J.H. Oldham. In the first book by a Christian leader on *Christianity and the Race Problem*, he had written already in 1924:

> Christianity is not primarily a philosophy but a crusade. As Christ was sent by the Father, so He sends His disciples to set up in the world the Kingdom of God. His coming was a declaration of war — a war to the death against the powers of darkness. He was manifested to destroy the works of the devil. Hence when Christians find in the world a state of things that is not in accord with the truth which they have learned from Christ, their concern is not that it should be explained but that it should be ended. In that temper we must approach everything in the relations between races that cannot be reconciled with the Christian ideal.

What Oldham said is as true for the 1980s as it was in the 1920s, and it is still a challenge too little heard.

The World Council and its member churches have gone through three phases in their combat against racism. The first phase began in Amsterdam and continued through the Evanston Assembly in 1954. A study was made in preparation for that assembly, based on the general question: "How can the church contribute to the correction of racial prejudice and injustice?" The topic at Evanston was: "Intergroup Relations — The Church Amid Racial and Ethnic Tensions." Historical, sociological, psychological, and theological aspects of racial and ethnic tensions were described, and a survey was made of positions which various churches had taken. The document which came out of the assembly was significant as the first effort by an ecumenical meeting to go beyond general statements and speak specifically to the churches about their responsibilities. Its resolution on racism was a definitive word:

> The Second Assembly of the World Council of Churches declares its conviction that any form of segregation based on race, colour, or ethnic origin is contrary to the gospel, and is incompatible with the Christian doctrine of man and with the nature of the Church of Christ. The Assembly urges the Churches within its membership to renounce all forms of segregation or discrimination

and to work for their abolition within their own life and within society.

The ongoing significance of this exercise was that it started a deep conversation within and among many churches. It was produced by Christians coming from many difficult racial situations, including representatives of churches in South Africa (three of which were later to withdraw their membership in the WCC). It made a major impact on the world scene. At the UN General Assembly meeting which followed the WCC assembly, this document was widely quoted with approval in speeches, not least by non-Christian delegates. Never before or since has a WCC statement been publicly acknowledged in this way in the sessions of the UN. However, the tone and content of the 1954 statement showed clearly that it was the voice of people speaking *for* the oppressed but without any profound solidarity *with* them. It failed to move beyond talking about the obvious manifestations of racism to an understanding of its underlying economic, political, and institutional roots. In the final analysis, it did not go much further than exhortation and pious hopes. The point I want to make, as one who participated in those discussions in the late 1940s and 1950s, is that many Christians and churches have not progressed beyond this early stage of the ecumenical debate and commitment. Some recent national and even regional reports, especially among those coming from North Atlantic countries, have much of the same Olympian tone and content as the Evanston resolution.

A second stage of the WCC's involvement in the struggle against racism was the period when there was a Secretariat on Racial and Ethnic Relations. Information about various situations was shared. Visits were made to trouble spots. Efforts were made to get churches to eliminate racial discrimination in their life and witness. Perhaps the test of this period were the consultations held in 1960, after the Sharpeville massacre, and in 1964. The emphasis of the first consultations was on how to maintain the fellowship between the white-dominated churches. The deep outrage of the brutally oppressed black people hardly found expression. In the second consultation there was an attempt to bring out the economic injustices which sustained racism, and the danger that the racially oppressed might resort to violence as the only way left to change their situation. An appeal was made to all parties, especially to the churches, to work for a racially just society. But again there was no clear tangible commitment to the oppressed themselves. Again, some of the reports during our present process of consultation still reflect this kind of general concern, emphasizing dialogue with church leadership and calls to action stimulated by fear of violent reaction by the racially oppressed.

The third stage started with the civil rights movement in the USA and the armed liberation struggle in southern Africa in the 1960s. The racially oppressed had begun taking their fate in their own hands. The nations, the racist oppressors, and the timid churches had to respond. For the WCC this happened at the Church and Society Conference in 1966 and at the Uppsala Assembly in 1968. But there had been other indications that a more profound understanding of racism and of the churches' role was developing. During the period between World War II and 1968, many countries of the Third World had become politically independent, but the economic and social structures of dependence, with strong racist overtones, remained and were even reinforced. The first decade of development had shown how economic imperialism was at the root of racism. The World Council's own study on Areas of Rapid Social Change, which led to the Church and Society Conference in 1966, and the establishment of the Commission on the Churches' Participation in Development, had prepared it for taking more affirmative action in solidarity with the oppressed themselves.

The Uppsala Assembly called for urgent and costly action by the World Council and its member churches. The following year the Programme to Combat Racism was launched, and the response to Oldham's call 25 years earlier for a crusade against racism became a combat. The scope and focus of this programme involved four convictions:

(1) Racism is a world phenomenon and takes different forms, including ethnocentrism, but by far the most flagrant and pervasive form of racism is white racism. The mandate states: "It is the coincidence, however, of an accumulation of wealth and power in the hands of the white peoples, following upon their historical and economic progress during the past 400 years, which is the reason for a focus on the various forms of *White*

Racism in the different parts of the world. People of different colour suffer from this Racism in all continents."

(2) Racism, and especially white racism, is reinforced by political, legal, economic, military, and social power structures which must be unmasked and challenged. These power structures are all the more demonic and entrenched because of the ideological and military confrontation of the great powers and their allies and satellites.

(3) Racism can only be combatted by the oppressed when they are empowered spiritually, economically, and politically. The Christian duty is, therefore, to express solidarity with the oppressed in all the ways compatible with our faith and in recognition of our own solidarity in the sin of racism.

(4) The churches, as expression both of the body of Christ the servant and of people who participate in the life of their societies, participate in the racist system either by active involvement or by passive complicity.

On the basis of these four convictions the WCC has been involved, with its member churches, in the struggle against racism in the light of God's purpose for humanity and creation. On that basis it will continue to be so involved.

### Ecumenical sharing of resources

Some twenty years ago I heard a Sudanese professor of history make a remark to a European visitor in Khartoum that I have never forgotten. "Remember that when you say 'history,'" the professor said, "you instinctively think back into what has passed into tradition and heritage. For us, history begins tomorrow." That remark haunts me whenever I hear the subject of "partnership in mission" being discussed: we have been talking about it for a very long time, but we have not advanced very far in doing something about it. The "history" of this kind of cooperation has yet to begin.

The Bangkok Assembly of the Commission on World Mission and Evangelism in 1972 was one of those rare ecumenical meetings in which participants said what we really thought. And the delegates' address to the question of partnership was candid: "Our basic problem is now to break free from the frustrating cycle of repeated statements which are received, filed, and not acted upon. Partnership in mission remains an empty slogan. Even where autonomy and equal partnership have been achieved in a formal sense, the actual dynamics remain such as to perpetuate relationships of dominance and dependence."

Already at the Edinburgh World Missionary Conference in 1910, much was said about how missionary societies and boards could cooperate in the evangelization of the world. However, out of the four hundred or so delegates present there were only seventeen from the so-called Third World, and they came as representatives of the Western missionary societies.

Twenty-eight years later the Madras Conference said:

> We believe that cooperation is in line with the will and purpose of God, and that it is thus essentially Christian. We would urge that not only between churches in each field but also in the relations between the older and the younger churches, cooperation should be regarded as the governing principle. In some cases, eagerness to cooperate among the younger churches is thwarted by a too-rigid control from abroad, and we cannot too strongly urge that such rigidity of control in this and other matters must be relaxed if the younger churches are to grow into fullness of Christian life and experience, and service.

It is interesting that this conference looked forward to the formation of the World Council of Churches as a means of promoting cooperation in mission; but it was only twenty-three years later that the International Missionary Council became integrated into the World Council of Churches at New Delhi. That in itself was a sign of the difficulty of coming to terms with cooperation and unity.

During World War II the mission-sending and giving countries were severely limited in dispatching money and people overseas. Yet at the end of the war, it was discovered that the churches in Asia, Africa, and the Pacific had grown in spite of the lack of missionary presence. Some of the sending countries themselves came out of the war with few resources. It was in that atmosphere that the Whitby Missionary Conference took place in 1947. Here the slogan "Partnership in Obedience" was coined, specifically referring to partnership in personnel, finance, policy, and administration. This was the first time the ecumenical movement expressed itself clearly on the issues of partnership for sharing.

Real partnership involves the grace of receiving as well as the grace of giving. Within the partnership, there is no reason why churches which are economically weak should hesitate to receive help from those which are economically strong. It is taken for granted that no Christian body will try to take advantage of its financial strength to secure dominance over any other. It is taken for granted also that receiving churches will be watchful against the danger that the availability of funds contributed by other partners may interfere with, or slow down the development of, their own plans of Christian stewardship.

When the World Council of Churches was formed, its Department on Christian Reconstruction and Inter-Church Aid was chiefly concerned with reconstruction and refugee service in Europe. By 1954 it had become the Division of Inter-Church Aid and Service to Refugees. Inter-Church Aid was seen as a permanent obligation of the World Council of Churches. "By accepting the privilege of sharing in this work," the Evanston Assembly said, "the member churches bear witness to their hope in Christ, and manifest the reality of the fellowship and the wholeness of the Church."

Between the Second and the Third Assemblies, a new element came to the fore. The Department on Church and Society launched a study on "Christian Responsibility in Areas of Rapid Social Change," directed mainly to Asia, Africa, and Latin America. The Madras Missionary Conference had discussed "The Economic Basis of the Church" and "The Church and the Changing Social and Economic Order," but it was this study on areas of rapid social change which really challenged the churches to partnership in world development. Its report in 1959 stated:

All peoples have a part to play in the development of the world. Those who have the resources and the skill can help others to develop, but they can only do this if they realize that all have gifts to contribute. Together, all need to learn to use the gifts they are given. Thus, they will learn to understand each other and work together for the glory of God and the help of each other.

Meanwhile the Division of Inter-Church Aid and Refugees extended its title to include World Service (CICARWS). In New Delhi CICARWS' mandate was formulated:

The churches which have covenanted together to manifest their underlying unity in Christ must seek to do this in every part of their life and this includes the sharing of their resources, both in personnel and materials.... Churches possessing resources do, in fact, secure new life and vision as they share their resources with others. Churches which are weak and struggling against great difficulties are encouraged and helped by the aid received, and more particularly by the knowledge that they are remembered in their need by fellow Christians.

The Uppsala Assembly in 1968 called the churches to action for world development:

The churches are already engaged in mission and service projects for economic and social development, and some of these resources could be used strategically on a priority basis for pioneer or demonstration projects, as an important response to the most acute need of specific peoples and areas. This would require a re-examination of the basic objectives of Church programmes and budgets in the light of urgent tasks of nation-building in developing countries. The churches should use their resources for God's purpose of abundant life for all. They should explore how international foundations could be set up through which endowments and other church funds may be responsibly invested for development.

In 1970 the Commission on the Churches' Participation in Development (CCPD) was set up. The purpose of development was seen as social justice through people's participation in decision-making and self-reliance in economic growth. It was emphasized that all societies are in process of development, so that all are both donors and receivers and therefore interdependent. Power must be distributed if the decision-making process is to be shared at all levels; and there must be coordination in planning and action in decision.

In some ways, these points reiterated what had been discussed in a more theoretical way by the churches concerned with mission in the 1940s and 1950s. But it was not until the 1970s that we were forced beyond generalities to face the real issues of the ecumenical sharing of resources. A series of events made this clear.

The first reality was that development aid resulted in the rich countries getting richer and the poor countries poorer. As we noted earlier this is a consequence of entrenched economic and political structures in both the giving and receiving countries, maintained through the transnational corporations and the growing militarization of society in a large number of countries of the world. What is true of governments and industrial enterprises is also true for the churches. Their structures of giving and receiving do not facilitate real partnership. Good will and fine statements are not enough to overcome this impediment: what is required is a rigorous examination of these structures.

Second, the issues of dominance and dependence, of power and powerlessness, have become clearer in recent years. The churches themselves are caught in this syndrome, especially as the churches of the rich countries continue to insist on bilateral relationships over against multilateral ecumenical ones, just as governments and corporations do. The response to this uncovering of dominance and dependence is that the poorer people have to learn the meaning and the means of gaining power. The issue has therefore become *empowering the powerless*. The initiatives have to be taken by the poor themselves.

The ecumenical movement has become involved in this in many different ways. In the Commission on World Mission and Evangelism, Urban Industrial Mission began developing people's movements in the 1960s. In Korea and the Philippines, these people's movements have come into a head-on clash with the authorities. The two points which have made the Programme to Combat Racism so controversial have been the fact that the grants are made on the basis of trust of the movements and groups to which they are made, and the fundamental and careful research which has been made of the anatomy of racist oppression. That careful research has uncovered how investments through corporations, banks, and others have reinforced the whole racist system, leaving the people no alternative but to struggle for their own liberation. This has given a focus and force to a good deal of other work going on in CCPD and elsewhere, including training programmes to prepare people for taking hold of their own fate and encouragement of appropriate technology.

Moreover, the WCC unit on Education and Renewal has been involved in programmes of participation in change. There have been educational reforms such as those associated with the name of Paulo Freire; there have been the women's liberation efforts; the scholarships programme; World Youth Projects, which has long history of promoting ecumenical exchange of resources, as well as the ecumenical work camps, now called the Ecumenical Youth Service.

The challenge today is that these efforts at empowering the powerless hardly touch the structures of churches in either rich or poor countries. They always seem to go around the issues of dominance and power. The churches themselves, with their strongly hierarchical structures, do not permit real participation by the whole people of God. A study by the Commission on World Mission and Evangelism on the "Missionary Structure of the Congregation" lamented what it called the church's "morphological fundamentalism" (only sociologists and theologians could produce such a phrase!) — that is to say, their attachment at all costs to structures handed down and preserved particularly by the power élites in the churches.

A third reality which has emerged in these years is the revolt against cultural imperialism: the insistence of Third World countries on their cultural identity rather than being considered as developing in the image of the rich industrialized countries. This has raised two issues for the churches. First, resources have been narrowly defined in terms of money, materials, and technically skilled persons, so that the people in the poorer countries were almost always put in the position of being on the receiving end. Their spiritual, theological, cultural, and human resources have not been considered, until recently, as something important to be shared. And yet it is precisely here that they can best offer assistance to the rich industrialized countries. Second, countries in the Third World have been asking for a moratorium on being recipients of money and people from the rich churches, so that they might discover their own priorities and resources and deploy them for mission and service. This would make for a more authentic relationship with other churches. Such a call for moratorium is not only in relation to churches and agencies outside of their country, but it is also addressed to the power élites in those churches, which have been a real hindrance to self-reliant decision-making in those churches. A moratorium of this kind would also enable the rich churches to rediscover priorities and use their resources for a more global approach to the task of mission and service at home and abroad.

These three issues have dominated ecumenical discussions during the past several years. The programme on Ecumenical Sharing of Resources is therefore the result of a long pilgrimage. Looking back over the past decades we can make a few summary observations.

First, there has been no problem in discussing ecumenically the nature and quality of relations of sharing between the churches. It has all been beautifully stated in document after document. After Edinburgh, the rich churches could no longer behave in an openly patronizing way, and they have tended to say all the right things. But the emphasis on finance and technical expertise has bedeviled the issues of sharing.

Second, so long as the churches were only concerned about their internal relations with each other, in mission and service, the issue of sharing did not come out sharply. Even in the Third World, especially in Asia, concern for church union as a means of effecting greater ecumenical sharing of resources has not produced the required results. Twenty-five years after the Church of South India had been in operation, a report about its life made one thing very clear: church union had not necessarily encouraged the ecumenical sharing of resources. The structures of support and the divisions of the churches in the sending countries did not encourage it; and church and institutional structures in South India itself were such that the aid remained bilateral. And even though the Church of North India has had many years to learn from the experience of the Church of South India, it has found it difficult indeed to try to establish ecumenical sharing of resources with eleven supporting agencies.

Only when the churches were forced to be concerned about questions of economic and social justice were their own inadequate structures of sharing exposed. The limited understanding of resources, the use of power and abuse of it, and the mechanisms which promote or hinder the ecumenical sharing of resources have been revealed. Thus the current programme emphasis on a just, participatory, and sustainable society is essential for the ecumenical sharing of resources.

Finally, the nerve of what we have to do lies in the structure of relationships. We have to ask what instruments and mechanisms we can put into motion to enable us all to empower the powerless and facilitate the sharing of all our resources ecumenically. Happily, there are signs that these mechanisms are being developed. Four things have to be borne in mind:

(1) There must be mechanisms and instruments to awaken the consciences of churches, agencies, and all persons involved.

(2) There must be mechanisms and instruments for promoting decision-making where the action has to be taken, and decision-making of all the parties involved.

(3) There must be programmes and experiments which break through the vicious circle of domination and dependence.

(4) There must be means for constant evaluation by the parties concerned.

Our task is to examine these mechanisms and instruments and see how we can go further on the road toward ecumenical sharing of resources.

### Science and technology

For a long time, the churches were notoriously shy about the issue of science and technology, reflecting a persistently negative attitude toward science as a result of a false interpretation of Scripture.

Nevertheless, the application of scientific methods to the criticism of the Bible since the nineteenth century has helped to bring about a more tolerant attitude in the churches toward science. That the Bible is not a book of science became evident. Scientific enquiry came to be viewed in the spirit of the biblical message that humanity is called to fulfil God's mandate to comprehend and master creation, to bring the unbridled forces of nature under human control, and to replenish the earth. All this is for "good," the well-being of all. During this century Christians have learned a great deal from science and scientists: rigorous and relentless examination to see what reality yields; the model of the commonwealth of science, which knows no national or ideological frontiers and in which there is a mutual sharing of ideas and discoveries and mutual correction where false turns in research have been detected; the monumental fruits of scientific enquiry and technological application which have transformed our world and opened up possibilities for a better life.

At the same time, scientists have become more modest in their claims. Albert Einstein agonized over the uses to which governments were putting the results of atomic research. After the bombings of Hiroshima and Nagasaki, it is reported that Nils Bohr hurried to his bishop in Copenhagen and exclaimed: "I have come to ask pardon for being alive." Scientists and technologists today are much more conscious of their social responsibility than in the past. Indeed, it is they who are now posing many of the most acute ethical questions to the churches and theologians, whose traditional categories of thinking are hardly adequate for such an enterprise.

This developing understanding between faith and science has led the ecumenical movement to devote more emphasis to the uses to which people put the artifacts of science-based technology. The ecumenical movement, which is concerned about the purpose of God for the *oikoumene*, has concentrated its attention on what kind of world of human beings is compatible with the gospel of the kingdom of God and his justice.

The 1925 Conference on Life and Work in Stockholm endorsed the aspirations of people for a "just and fraternal order, through which the opportunity shall be assured for the development, according to God's design, of the full manhood of every man." There is not much difference between this stated goal and the current WCC programme emphasis on a just, participatory, and sustainable society.

In 1928 the International Missionary Council gave much attention to "the Christian mission in relation to industrial problems in Asia and Africa." It said: "The Christian will welcome the triumphs of science and technical skill by which the resources which God has given to his children have been made more fully available for the service of all. But he will regard material wealth as an instrument, not as an end.... He will desire that economic interests shall be, not the master, but the servant of civilization."

The 1937 Oxford Conference on Church, Community and State, had much to say about the existing economic order, which had revealed its true character through successive technological improvements. This conference declared:

It was thought at one time that the development of this new economic order would not only improve the material conditions of life but would also establish social justice. This expectation was rooted in the belief that a pre-established harmony would so govern the self-interest of individuals as to create the greatest possible harmony of society as a whole. "Each man, seeking his own, would serve the commonwealth." Today this belief is largely discredited.... The same forces which had produced material progress have often enhanced inequalities, created permanent insecurity, and subjected all members of modern society to the domination of so-called independent economic "laws."... Industrial expansion and technical progress have tended to defeat their own ends.... Christians have a particular responsibility to make whatever contribution they can towards the transformation, and if necessary the thorough reconstruction, of the present economic and political system.

In those early years of ecumenical social thought, science-based technology was always related to the aims and actual performance of economic and political systems. The First Assembly of the WCC spoke of the contribution of the "undirected developments of technology" to the disorder of society. In the following years ecumenical discussion paid increasing attention to the role of science and technology in shaping and reinforcing the power structures of society. The World Conference on Church and Society in 1966 stated:

Technological society is based on a continuous and consistent process of change which affects all men. It leads to a concentration of power in the hands of relatively few with the danger of its misuse by privileged groups and the destruction of democracy by a decision-making technocracy. At the same time, as technological change advances, its complexity demands interdependence and cooperation. If technological change is to serve human needs, the rate of change must be governed by a primary consideration for human welfare....

At its best, technology can be part of man's historic search for truth and justice, and from this search it derives its real meaning.... Political power plays a crucial role in determining the pace and purpose of technological development. Today such power is exercised not only by public officials but also by technologists, even though they may be reticent to admit it. When technologists advise politicians or make policy themselves, they are making political decisions and must do so within a just and viable decision-making system.... We suggest that the just and humane use of technology requires that every individual participate in the decision-making system to a degree commensurate with his capacity to do so.

Two years later the Uppsala Assembly of the World Council bravely launched an appeal for rapid world development through the transfer of technology from the rich to the poorer nations. As we saw earlier, it soon became apparent that this was an inadequate way of proceeding, because it left the unjust structures of society and of relations between nations untouched. The 1974 world conference on Science and Technology for Human Development recognized the problem and spoke of the "need for the invention of social mechanisms which will enable science and technology to serve social justice at all levels." At the Nairobi Assembly a strong warning note was struck:

> It is the considered view of many scientists and technologists that the world is on a catastrophic course leading to mass starvation, global depletion of resources, and global environmental deterioration. The responsibility that now confronts humanity is to make a deliberate transition to a sustainable global society in which science and technology will be mobilized to meet the basic physical and spiritual needs of people, minimize human suffering, and to create an environment which can sustain a decent quality of life for all people. This will involve a radical transformation of civilization, new technologies, new uses for technology, and new global and political systems.

It was in the light of this long development of thought on the place of science and technology that the 1979 conference in Cambridge, Massachusetts, on Faith, Science, and the Future fit into the framework of the WCC's overall programme emphasis on a just, participatory, and sustainable society. The issues of faith and science must be seen concretely in that context. Any attempt to articulate afresh a doctrine of creation and of humanity must be done in the context both of God's revelation in history and of the actualities and longings of creation and humanity in history.

There can be no doubt about the profound contribution of science and technology in alerting us to the urgent necessity of creating "a sustainable global society in which science and technology will be mobilized to meet the basic physical and spiritual needs of society." There can be no just society which is not sustainable, that is, which does not nourish a creation which provides the means by which people can truly share the inheritance of the earth, so that all can live and maintain themselves in freedom and community. But we must at the same time face the limitations of science and technology as they are carried out at present.

The report to the Club of Rome, *Reshaping the International Order*, under the guidance of the Dutch economist Jan Tinbergen, states:

> Nowhere is the disparity between the industrialized and third world countries more marked than in the field of scientific research and technological development. Although 90% of all the technologists and scientists that have ever lived are alive today, over 90% are at work in the industrialized countries. Over 90% of their activities are concentrated on research for the rich world and on converting their findings into protected technical processes. The rich minority thus commands an overwhelming proportion of techno-scientific development.

Furthermore, it is said that over 50% of scientists and technologists are engaged in arms research and development. Arms production wastes the resources of the earth. It takes away from the production of goods which would meet the needs of the people. And since such arms research and development is carried out in secret, its true cost is hidden from the people.

Who decides how the resources for scientific research and development are apportioned and how the results are used? The general impression one gets is that only governments and big corporations can provide the necessary funds and facilities. How free then are scientists and technologists? The traditional posture of scientists is that they can only work in freedom with the results of their work being made public. Their *raison d'être* is the search for truth in the Greek sense of *aletheia*, that which is not hidden and confined but disclosed and open for all to see; or in the Hebrew sense of *'emeth*, that which is true to itself, trustworthy, faithful to one's being.

The Hebrew for righteousness, justice — *sedeq* — means the ability to maintain oneself, to act according to one's nature, to have firmness and strength, integrity of character. Applied to society, it refers to mutual acknowledgment of persons, mutual maintenance of each other's honour and integrity, enabling one another to maintain themselves and to play their full part in the life of the covenant community. Truth and justice are therefore closely related, as the Psalmist sings: "Truth will spring up from the ground, and righteousness, justice, will look down from the sky. Yea, the Lord will give what is good, and our land will yield its increase" (Ps. 85:11-12). Sustainability depends on truth and justice and the gift of what is good. It has been rightly said that "the good" is that which increases communication and multiplies responsibilities.

In other words, a just and sustainable society is impossible without a society which is participatory, and science and technology today are not really participatory. They are forced to be biased on the side of those who wield economic and political power, which means against the oppressed, deprived, and marginalized — the people. Science and technology might claim to be objective and universal, but this claim is not borne out in reality. The whole drift of ecumenical social thought, especially in recent years, is that participation in decision-making is an essential dimension in the cause of justice for all and for fullness of life for all.

But what does participation concretely mean within the highly complex situation of science and technology? Let me give a few examples.

In 1965 the executive committee of the World Student Christian Federation met at the Massachusetts Institute of Technology. We were trying to understand how that world-renowned institution works. One celebrated professor in the social sciences told us of a research project he and his colleagues had undertaken for the US government. They were asked to study certain trouble spots during those stormy years of the civil rights movement. They chose the Watts area in Los Angeles and predicted that, in view of the total situation of discontent, which they described in detail, there would be riots during the hot summer. The report was duly submitted to the government. Nothing was done about it. The riots took place, as predicted. Could that report not have been given to the public by the professor, or at least to those in California, both black and white, who could have done something about it? The professor was himself convinced that had there been participation of a wide variety of people at different levels of power something could indeed have been done.

The churches in recent years have been talking a great deal about the acceleration of arms production and of the arms race. This is the field in which scientists and technologists today are most involved. They know what is going on. They know how resources are wasted and they recognize the need to switch arms industries into socially viable projects. Research institutes and special sessions of the UN have demonstrated that if communities were better informed and allowed to express themselves on options for their nations, there could be a way of halting the arms race and achieving genuine disarmament. After all, the decisions about arming are taken by human beings. Disarmament could also be willed by human beings. What is the role of science and technology in helping to demystify the situation and dispelling the widespread feeling of helplessness and hopelessness?

It is well known that scientists and technologists disagree about the safety of nuclear power stations. It is equally evident that the problems are probably soluble. Nevertheless, people have been kept in ignorance about the hazards involved. They have not had a chance to discuss the issues and make responsible decisions about them. Therefore when accidents occur both the authorities and the scientific establishment are called into question. The WCC sub-unit on Church and Society has striven to bring together a wide variety of people, including top scientists, and to stimulate discussion in Christian perspective on the options before people. The debate has been fierce, but it is a genuine debate about real issues.

The WCC has also been heavily involved in a programme called Urban and Industrial Mission, with over 2500 contact groups around the world — groups of workers or unemployed who organize themselves in people's movements to affirm their rights to work, to a decent wage, to adequate living and working conditions, and to a technology appropriate for meeting their needs. But throughout this programme it has proved extremely difficult to have any viable dialogue with the town and industrial planners and the science-based technologists. This invariably brings about frustration and anger, with the powers using harsh methods to silence the people. Again, science and technology are seen by the people to be on the side of oppression and injustice.

Medical science has tended to concentrate on sophisticated and expensive health-care centres and expertise. But it is estimated that, especially in the poorer countries of the world, only about 7% of the community is served by the hospitals in which all this equipment and expertise are located. The WCC's Christian Medical Commission has been experimenting with community health care, which includes involving the people themselves in delivering health care as far as their knowledge and experience will permit, using and improving local medicines, through medical science and concentrating on the people as a healing community. This is an example of how participation of both the community and medical scientists can transform the situation of health and healing, especially when coupled with the participation of the people in their own development in self-reliance.

These stories illustrate the need for participation as a way of sharing power toward a more just and sustainable society. Science and technology are not neutral or value-free, but are instruments of power, and that means political power. The central issue is how science and technology can become the vehicles, not for legitimizing and perpetuating structures of injustice, but for opening up the possibilities for structures of social control, which include all the people.

Faith is first of all a call to repentance, *metanoia*, a radical change in our thinking and outlook, our style of life, indeed, our whole being. We saw earlier in this book how that means a turning toward God in Christ and toward our fellow human beings. It is an act of sharing in the death of Christ — the crucifixion of our self-regarding existence. And it is an act of sharing in the resurrection of Christ — the affirmation of the impossible becoming real, of life being wrested from death. Faith in the crucified and risen Lord is, therefore, a radical break with a static understanding of our existence into dynamic living and daring God's future. To have faith is to hope and to act in hope through love. Such faith, hope, and love liberate us to struggle for a just, participatory, and sustainable society. That is our calling as Christians and as scientists and technologists.

# 7. A worldwide fellowship

For more than thirty years I have been deeply involved in the life and work of the ecumenical movement. It was at the Second World Conference of Christian Youth in Oslo in 1947 that I had my first real exposure to the sufferings and hopes of people around the world. As I reflect on the years since then, I am gratified by how much more sensitive Christians have become to the pain which is the daily lot of other people in the world and how often they have entered courageously into the struggle of others for justice and humanity, realizing that it is our struggle too.

In the previous chapters we have touched on a number of programmatic emphases through which the World Council of Churches has sought to incarnate the vision of the unity of the body of Christ which has activated the modern ecumenical movement. Now I should like to conclude by developing some of the human insights which we in the ecumenical movement have seen — sometimes more, sometimes less clearly. At many points, what we have to say in these last two chapters will touch upon and cut across earlier parts of the book. It will also, I hope, suggest directions and emphases for the future.

We have learned a great deal from the experience of these years. In the beginning it was the biblical renewal movement of the 1930s and 1940s in Europe and North America that was the focal point for our thinking and action. We learned from Richard Niebuhr and others to have the Bible in one hand and the newspaper in the other: the Bible providing the criterion of understanding events, and the newspaper helping us appreciate the relevance and contemporary character of the Bible. In this context the prophets and the Jesus of history became alive for us. We saw that the kingdom of God had to do with his justice, not only in making the individual sinner righteous but also in calling for a reordered society in which the fruits of creation were shared with all. This in turn enabled us to read with discernment the literature which has poured out from a variety of ideological perspectives, and thus to enter into the struggle for a responsible society.

Examining the injustices of our times has led us into a variety of programmes in a number of areas. Over the years there has been a distinct move from declarations and educational efforts to action/reflection programmes. Throughout there have been strenuous attempts to challenge the churches to be *the church* — the pilgrim people of God. The church must move from its institutional ghetto and become a mobile witness and servant in the world. Time and again we have stressed that the church is the *laos*, the laity, the whole people of God, who must be engaged in making God's sovereign love known in every sphere of life, and in each place. The selfhood and integrity of the church must come to expression in and enter into dialogue with each culture.

## Suffering and hope

One specific facet of the human experience to which we have been increasingly exposed in the ecumenical movement is suffering. In many parts of our world the experience of Christians is precisely the experience of suffering; and for many people with whom we confess a common faith, the search for hope must be carried on in a context which seems to promise only despair and death. It is only when we have listened to the voices of such people that we can presume even to begin speaking about a biblical view of suffering. Such modesty has not always characterized Christians who have spoken and written on this subject.

Suffering has been regarded as punishment for sin, as a test sent by God, or as an inevitable mystery which must be endured in hope of eternal life after death. Because of the measure of truth in these conceptions of suffering, they retain an attraction for many Christians.

It is true that when we rebel against God's will and way for our lives, when we assert ourselves over against God and our fellows, the result is suffering, not only for ourselves but for others. Of course, it does not necessarily follow that those who do evil suffer. John Calvin, when asked about the observed fact that the ungodly seem to flourish, answered: "Because the Lord is fattening them up like pigs for the slaughter." History indicates that in the end the ungodly do come to grief, but in the meantime they cause a great deal of grief for others. But what does that say about God? Is this the God of our Lord Jesus Christ? Is it his way to stand aside and let the wicked work out suffering in the world until they overreach themselves?

These arguments have been extended to try to explain away the sufferings of people. Poverty, slavery, and deprivation are seen as the result of some wrong in people who could not fend for themselves. The blacks in North America and southern Africa have been relegated to being the sons and daughters of Ham, cursed. Tyrants could not be overthrown because they were left to the good pleasure of God. In this connection theologians have even invoked original sin, which is always with us. We may be saved individually from sin, but not from sufferings. The soul may be saved, but the body is left to the oppressor. It is astonishing how often such arguments and convictions have been used to justify the *status quo* and the survival of the fittest.

Similarly, the idea that suffering is a test from God to purify us has some element of truth in it. But purify us for what? Why suffering as a means of purifying? The story of Job is a classic on this point. None of the well-crafted rational arguments of his friends can persuade Job that the suffering inflicted on him is God's purpose. If it is, then Job appeals to God against God. Here again, the idea of suffering as a test has been used as a means of incapacitating people from revolting against unwarranted suffering. Again and again oppressed people have been given this cold comfort. Blacks in Africa, North America, and the Caribbean, Indians in North and South America, and the peoples of Asia were expected to see their sufferings as a purifying test from God. They were even given the accolade of virtue if they meekly accepted their lot. Their simple faith was applauded — always by those who profited from their situation.

Another common conviction is that human suffering is an insoluble mystery to which only death can bring an end. Hope is seen in life after death. Suffering is, indeed, a mystery. But has God left us to hope only in the life to come? If so, there is no meaning in entering into the sufferings of others now.

None of these views of suffering is, of course, held in so crude a form by churches today. But remnants of these attitudes and corresponding practices show that they still persist deep within us, and they inhibit us from genuine struggling against people's suffering.

Behind these views of suffering lies an understanding of a God who is wholly other, transcendent, uninvolved, and incapable of pain. The life and mission of Jesus become an embarrassment for such an understanding of God; and some strange theologies have been concocted to explain away his passion and death on the cross. This gulf between God's presumed painlessness, apathy, and the sufferings of Christ takes away a great deal of the immediate relevance of God's revelation in Christ for our struggle aginst suffering and for a hope which can free people from unnecessary suffering now.

The theologies which have come out of the struggles of Christians in the last twenty years or so question this understanding of God in terms of his revelation in the Bible and of the experience of people who have lived the word of God. Here I can indicate only briefly some of what we have learned in these years of tested experience of suffering and hope.

(1) American blacks have taught us to sing in their spirituals that God is the God of the oppressed, the God who heard the cry of the enslaved people of Israel and liberated them from Egypt. He is Yahweh, the one who is present with his people. The Exodus faith has been the mainstay of the existence of black people. Even if generation after generation suffered at the hands of their oppressors, they had a deep awareness of God's presence with them. That awareness was reinforced as they accepted by faith Jesus Christ, who came to bring liberty to the captives and did so with his own life. His resurrection has been for them the assurance of God's victory now and to come. Therefore they can carry on the struggle with the invincible

spirit of those who have overcome suffering. They will not allow themselves to be discouraged or left voiceless, numb, and in despair. Martin Luther King continued to have a dream of liberation for all even when he knew he would be assassinated. It was a dream, a hope solidly based in the God who is true to his promises.

The inner conquest of suffering is hope in action, and is the indispensable preparation for fighting against the causes of suffering.

(2) Latin American Christians, both Roman Catholic and Protestant, have been experiencing afresh the challenge of the prophets to suffering. They have found that the assault on suffering begins when people's awareness of their suffering is aroused and they no longer remain in apathy and silence. Hence the emphasis on conscientization — enabling people to think with the whole of themselves and to see each other as subjects and not as objects.

Jeremiah set out to open people's eyes to their suffering and to the suffering they cause. He did that in the name of God's justice, his covenant call to his people to build and plant his creation for all to share. Although he encountered the implacable hatred of the political leaders, he did not become silent. He complained to God:

> Just art thou, O Lord, when I complain to thee
> yet I would plead my case before thee.
> Why does the way of the wicked prosper?
> Why do all who are treacherous flourish? (12:1).

God's answer is not direct. What comes through is the compulsion on Jeremiah to go on speaking the word of justice:

> O Lord, thou hast deceived me,
> and I was deceived;
> thou art stronger than I,
> and thou hast prevailed....
> For whenever I speak, I cry out,
> I shout, "Violence and destruction!"
> For the word of the Lord has become for me
> a reproach and derision all day long.
> If I say, "I will not mention him,
> or speak any more in his name,"

> there is in my heart as it were a burning fire
> shut up in my bones,
> and I am weary with holding it in,
> and I cannot (20:7-9).

That word is the new covenant which binds people to God in the intimacy of a knowledge which redeems and equips them for confronting suffering (Jer. 31:31-34). It also enables them to defeat their oppressors in exile by their organization of a just community life:

> Build houses and live in them: plant gardens and eat their produce.... Seek the peace (well-being) of the city where I have sent you into exile, and pray to the Lord on its behalf, for in its peace (well-being) you will find peace (well-being) (29:5,7).

A second insight into suffering from the Christians of Latin America has to do with the fact that theology, the understanding of God and his ways, does not come from a theoretical study of God's being or from philosophical enquiry. We cannot wait for God's answer to all our questions before we do his work. It is in our obedience in *praxis*, the critical relationship between our questioning and our actions in the midst of human anguish, that we discover what God is saying to us. Moreover, this *praxis* is concerned with making God's covenant justice alive among people who suffer and those who cause suffering. And this is done, as the prophets and especially Jeremiah did, by a radical analysis of the causes of suffering and the determination to eradicate those causes.

So it was with Jesus. When John the Baptist sent to ask him a thoroughly theological question, "Are you he who is to come or shall we look for another?" Jesus replies:

> Go and tell John what your hear and see: the blind receive their sight and the lame walk, lepers are cleansed and the deaf hear, and the dead are raised up, and the poor have good news preached to them. And blessed is he who takes no offense at me (Matt. 11:4-6).

God in Christ is known by what he does and his is a work of liberation from suffering.

(3) Asian theology has been teaching us to enter into the pain of God. A pioneering book in this area was *The Pain of God* by Kazoh Kitamori of Japan. This and other works have reminded

us that God was in Christ taking upon himself the sufferings of his creation. He was himself involved with us, participating in our pain. But he has done that to bring about our liberation in love and justice.

The "Servant of the Lord" in Second Isaiah is the chosen one, the delight of God, who goes forth in the Spirit and enabling power of God to bring justice to the nations. He upholds the weak. Immediately after the first Servant song (Isa. 42:1-4) the word of the Lord is:

> I am the Lord, I have called you in justice
> I have taken you by the hand and kept you;
> I have given you as covenant to the people,
> a light to the nations,
> to open the eyes that are blind,
> to bring out the prisoners from the dungeon,
> from the prison those who sit in darkness.
> I am the Lord, that is my name;
> my glory I give to no other,
> nor my praise to graven images.
> Behold, the former things have come to pass,
> and new things I now declare:
> before they spring forth I tell you of them.

The pain of God through his Servant is the birth pangs of new things which express God's justice. The last Servant Song (Isa. 52:13-53:12) portrays the Servant taking on our pain and sufferings, but in a way which purifies us from those pains which our sins have inflicted on us. And he accounts us just. It is this solidarity with the sufferers, this taking upon himself our sufferings which is the message of hope.

Jesus incarnates the servant of the prophet's vision. In Gethsemane he expresses the full weight of suffering. Suffering is not something to be embraced for the morbid fun of it, but it is to be borne in order to bear it away. The Russian liturgy has a word on this:

> Everyone who helps another is Gethsemane,
> Everyone who comforts another is the mouth of Christ.

When Masao Takenaka says "God is rice," I understand him to be speaking of the pain of God, especially as expressed by Christ: "If any one eats this bread (rice), he will live for ever, and the bread (rice) which I shall give is my flesh for the life of the world" (John 6:51). This is what is meant by the sacramental nature of our faith: "My Body given for you; my Blood shed for you." When we have learned to say and live those words to and with the people, we are sharing truly the pain of God which heals the pain of men and women.

I take this to be the meaning of that tremendous passage in Romans 8:1. We are only children of God and heirs with Christ as we share his sufferings and so become the means of the liberation of all creation. But this is only possible as the Spirit empowers us to address God and as we know that we are inseparable from his love, whatever befalls us in our participation in his pain.

(4) Finally, the churches are learning together from Orthodox liturgy, spirituality, and theology, that suffering and hope find their meaning and their creative power in the resurrection of Christ. When we are raised with Christ a revolution takes place in us. Those things which cause suffering to others and ourselves are put to death, and we assume a new nature which is being renewed in knowledge after the Creator. The divisions of our world, which cause so much suffering, are conquered; and we are clothed with those qualities which can make that conquest real (Col. 3:1-14). This was Paul's experience when he found that all he considered precious, everything which led him to be a persecutor, became nothing to him so that he might know Christ "and the power of his resurrection and the fellowship of his sufferings" (Phil. 3:8-10). It is in the power of the resurrection that we can share the sufferings of Christ on behalf of our fellow human beings.

Suffering and hope find their true meaning in Jesus Christ, our crucified and risen Lord. Only in him can we as his body be enabled and empowered to take on the sufferings of our fellow human beings and bring the hope of God's justice and peace to them in word and deed.

*Participation: the challenge and call*

Much of the suffering in our world touches those who are disenfranchised, those who do not have the right to share in the decisions which affect their life and their livelihood. The sense of being at the mercy of forces over which one cannot exercise the slightest control cuts across lines of race and class and geography and wealth, from corporate boardroom to peasant hovel, from government palace to prison camp — though of course it is the poor and downtrodden for whom its effects are usually the most immediate and devastating.

Here, too, the experience of the ecumenical movement has shown us more clearly a facet of the human predicament which surely calls for more than a programmatic address. Christians working together must listen with increasingly sensitive ears to the cries for participation which sound in our world today. These cries take many forms. There is the demand for participation in the decision-making process in industry and the economy, in complex but far-reaching areas like nuclear energy, genetics, and social planning. There is the search for cultural identity and self-reliance through people's power in situations where people have too long been treated as the consumers of dominant cultures, ideologies, and techniques rather than as producers according to their own culture and capacities. There is the determination to share more equitably in the earth's resources and the fruits of one's labour. The current concern for human rights is another expression of the challenge to participation.

As the Nairobi Assembly of the WCC observed, one answer to the worldwide call for participation has been suppression, often by violent means. "This in turn provokes counter-violence, which is called terrorism." In response, there has been a "steady erosion of private and public liberties in East and West, in North and South."

> The whole world is caught in a profound conflict between those who yearn and struggle to participate in change for a more humane existence and those who seek to maintain the *status quo* of power relations whether their ideology is capitalist or socialist — between people wanting to share power to shape the future and people holding on to power that shaped the past.

The existing structures of relationships, of the ordering of society, and of inherited or imposed values are admittedly complex. The cry for participation is only the announcement of a challenge to clear and deep analysis and to a process of reflection nourished by action for greater participation. What guidance does our Christian faith give us as we seek to face that challenge to participation today? What is our calling as Christians?

Participation has its source in God's covenant relationship with people. He liberated Israel from the oppression of Egypt and set them on a course to a land where they could carry out his purpose of fulfilling creation for good. He therefore invited them into a covenant; and this covenant has as its content the law or teaching which is concerned about their total allegiance to him as Creator and Saviour and their total commitment to one another. This covenant was to include all humanity. That was their mission.

The prophets gave further content to the participation of the covenant people of God as they spoke to the realities of Israel's life in the midst of the nations. They enriched the content of God's law or teaching as they challenged the people to act in justice, steadfast love, truth, faithfulness, and peace. All that denies people the right and privilege of participating in the life and purpose of God is a denial of the covenant — sin *par excellence.* Isaiah's vision of the messianic covenant is that the exercise of justice and equity will bring about the full participation of creation with human beings in an earth full of the knowledge of God (Isa. 11:1-9). When Jeremiah spoke about the new covenant he emphasized the personal responsibility of everyone as participating in the knowledge of his will and in making that will known (Jer. 31:27-34).

This new covenant was made incarnate in Jesus Christ. His message was the kingly rule of God and his justice. All are invited to share the life of the covenant and to participate in God's purpose for the world. Jesus himself showed the way to such participation by self-giving love. No one is excluded from God's kingdom — the children, the poor, the outcasts, the sick in body and mind. These must all be enabled to participate as human beings made in God's image. And the mark of the covenant is the eucharistic blessing: "My body given for you; my blood shed for you."

Paul makes this participation central in his letters to the Corinthians: "The cup of blessing which we bless, is it not a participation in the blood of Christ? The bread which we break, is it not a participation in the body of Christ? Because there is one loaf, we who are many are one body, for we all partake of the same loaf" (1 Cor. 10:16-17). Paul develops this participation in the Body of Christ by reminding us that each part of the body has its own integrity, its own distinctiveness, its own subjectivity, and that all parts of the body need each other. We all receive varied gifts, but the gift which unites us, without which our other gifts are uncreative, is the gift of love. Love links us all in an all-including covenant fellowship. That is the heart of participation (1 Cor. 12 and 13).

Furthermore, the mission of the people of God is seen as the building up of the Body of Christ and the attainment of unity in faith and in the knowledge of the Son of God leading to the fullness of our humanity in love. This mission calls for the full participation of all the members. The growth of the body of Christ cannot be the work of only apostles, prophets, evangelists, and teachers. It must come from all the members — and that means men and women, younger and older, pastors and laity, Jew and Gentile (Eph. 4; Gal. 3:27-28; Col. 3:9-14).

It is as a result of listening to this prominent theme in the biblical message and comparing this ideal with the reality of our world that the ecumenical movement has focused on participation from the very beginning. We saw in the previous chapter that the consequence of this concern has been fine-sounding talk rather than courageous action rather more often than we should hope. Nevertheless, the challenge to us today is to move beyond the shortcomings of the past, not merely to document them. We must reaffirm what the International Missionary Council said in Whitby in 1947 about partnership in obedience, which involves "the grace of receiving as well as the grace of giving." We must seek new ways to make the declaration of the Amsterdam Assembly about the "whole church with the whole gospel to the whole person in the whole world" more than a slogan. We must incorporate genuine participation, worldwide, into the insistence of the Evanston Assembly in 1954 that "clergy and laity belong together in the church; if the church is to perform her mission in the world they need each other."

In the 1950s and 1960s, as we have seen, the WCC engaged in intensive discussions on areas of rapid social change and on Christian witness in urban, industrial, and rural situations.

Many programmes emerged from these discussions. The experience of the churches in this field showed how development involves much more than economic growth. Much more important in the process of human development is the search for social justice and self-reliance, which cannot be undertaken without people's participation. The option for people's participation has led many churches, especially in Africa, Asia, and Latin America, to carry on their theological reflection in the context of participation: people's movements, people's parishes, and so on. Theology is nourished by involvement and action, and this inductive method of doing theology has in turn contributed to the ecumenical dialogue of the churches today. We had a glimpse of that in the preceding section, when we saw how Asian theology of suffering and hope, Latin America theology of liberation, and black theologies in Africa and the USA can help to move us beyond a sterile, intellectual, and finally unsatisfying approach to the suffering in the world. The "grassroots communities" that play a vital role in the process of church renewal are intimately related to these theological developments.

The call for a moratorium of funds and personnel issued at the Bangkok Assembly of the WCC Commission on World Mission and Evangelism in 1973 was fundamentally an appeal for the churches to participate in mission in their own situation. This call was particularly relevant to the churches in Africa, and the next year the Assembly of the All Africa Conference of Churches appealed to dependent churches to discover their own resources, which cannot be money or expatriate personnel, but basically their membership. The call for a moratorium must be understood as the call *to be the church*, rooted and incarnate in a given culture, and participating in God's mission in that culture and beyond.

We have referred more than once to the priority given by the WCC at its Nairobi Assembly to the search for a just, participatory, and sustainable society. Christians are called to proclaim and witness to the kingdom of God and his justice. This justice can only become real as all participate in the life of society and the resources of the earth are sustained and replenished for the use and well-being of all. This involves a diversity of programmes, such as the search for a new international economic order in the context of the structures of injustice, the role of science and technology for promoting a just society, the promotion of human rights, militarism and the armaments race as obstacles to participation and people's power, urban and industrial mission, community health care, and an authentic partnership of women and men in society.

The challenge and call of partnership is an integral part of the gospel. But the churches cannot promote participation in society unless they practice participation in their life. Where the structures of the churches' preaching, teaching, and witness are hierarchical, there is little room for the full participation of the whole people of God. The ecumenical movement has been challenging the churches for the last thirty years to renew their life so that there can be real participation in the body of Christ, for the life of the world. God's design is that all human beings may be included in his realm of power and love.

*Experiencing God around the world*

One of the benefits of increased participation which we have seen in the ecumenical movement is the exposure of people to the incredibly rich variety which characterizes the human experience of God. The experience of God is, of course, an intensely personal reality, which does not lend itself to being set forth in a systematic fashion. We can only reflect on the experience of God and catch a glimpse of the wealth of his being through the varied ways in which people in their particularities have been grasped by him.

For that reason I should like in this section to evoke my own experience and that of some of my contemporary fellow-pilgrims in black America, Africa, Latin America, and Asia. In order for this experience to be shared in its widest sense, what is needed is a true dialogue between cultures. Let me begin by indicating briefly the terms involved here.

First, when I speak of God it is of the God made known to us in the history of the people of Israel and supremely in Jesus Christ. Second, the call for dialogue is used not to refer to an academic and intellectual exercise, but to the meeting of life with life, the encounter of persons, in openness and mutual respect, at the deepest levels of their existence. Third, I use culture in the way Jürgen Moltmann employs it in his book *The*

*Church in the Power of the Spirit*: "The sphere of the self-representation of persons, groups and peoples in relation to one another and as a whole before the ground of their existence." What I like about this definition is that it assumes the necessity of intercourse between persons, groups, and peoples out of the particularities of their total life in one inhabited earth, *oikoumene*, particularities which arise out of their intercourse with the ground of their existence, the Lord of the *oikoumene* (Psalm 24:1 in the Greek Old Testament). "The history of the world," Martin Buber says, "is a real dialogue between God and his creature."

\* \* \*

And so I start with my experience of God in the context of my own Caribbean culture. When Christopher Columbus reached land in the Caribbean, his first act was to set up a cross. He called the island San Salvador (Holy Saviour or Liberator). We in the islands often remark that Columbus planted the cross and we have been carrying it ever since. The first to bear the cross were the people he found there: Arawaks in the north, Caribs in the south, both Mongolian peoples. In twenty-five years of Spanish rule it is believed that some three million died from the slavery to which they were subjected.

Then followed the slave trade from the west coast of Africa — a trade which went on until the early nineteenth century. Slaves were brought to the Caribbean and the coast of Latin America and later to North America. Estimates are that only one-tenth of the thirty million slaves captured during these centuries ever arrived. We are descendants of those who survived. The Caribbean became the hunting ground of pirates, adventurers of all sorts: scions of aristocratic families, escaping debtors and criminals from Europe, white indentured labourers, and, after black slavery, Asian Indian and Chinese indentured labourers.

Spanish, British, Dutch, and French colonies were set up and vied with each other for sovereignty over the islands, reflecting their own struggles in Europe. The remnant of the indigenous people, the slaves and indentured labourers, were the least considered in this context. Christianity came in various forms to the islands — first Roman Catholics, later the main confessions of the Reformation. But those who first came did so in search of gold and of souls, in that order. The Caribbean was the testing ground of colonialism, imperialism, capitalist racism. After nearly five hundred years, we Caribbeans are experienced in most of the ills our world suffers in the encounter of peoples and cultures.

My own island was discovered on a Sunday, hence its name "Dominica." But what we are most aware of is not the memory of the celebration of the Lord's Day, the day of resurrection and newness of life, but of the slaughter of the Caribs by the invading French in 1750, the first foreign power to occupy the island. Dominica's ferocious Caribs held out longer than anyone else in the Caribbean, thanks to the mountainous character of the island; and the intensity of the French victory is reflected today in the name of the site where it took place — a village now called Massacre.

In the eighteenth century, Moravians, Baptists, and Methodists began to preach the gospel in the Caribbean. For the British territories emancipation came on August 1, 1834. The slaves received their freedom in acts of worship at which the words of Paul were read: "For freedom Christ has set us free; stand fast therefore, and do not submit again to a yoke of slavery" (Gal. 5:1).

When I was born, Christianity in its most traditional confessional forms reigned supreme in the Caribbean, except for two or three places where Asian Indians remained as Hindus and Muslims. Like my fellow islanders I was born in the bosom of the church and went through all the conventional motions to which so many throughout the world are accustomed. We were taught about a God of love, our Father in heaven, made known to us in Jesus Christ. But I remember the crisis I went through at the age of nine in 1930 when we had our third hurricane in my short life. Our whole economy was destroyed and with it whatever wealth some of our families had enjoyed. Moreover, we were already caught in the world economic depression.

It was in this situation of inherited tragedy and the needless suffering and meaninglessness of our existence that God became a reality for me — a reality which I experienced in my obsession with the crucified Christ. Faith was for me the great "in spite of". God was not indifferent to our lot. He assumed it himself. Paul's letter to the Philippians became a sheet anchor for me, especially chapter 2 which speaks of Christ becoming a slave (*doulos*) for our sake. Another word of Paul which impressed itself on me as a teenager was his reminder to the Corinthian church: "You know the grace of our Lord Jesus Christ, that though he was rich, yet for your sake he became poor, so that by his poverty you might become rich" (2 Cor. 8 :9).

My experience was by no means unique. I was heir to the "in spite of" faith of my people. It was the air I breathed — though the air was not by any means always clean. Perhaps our basic attitude is illustrated by two calypso spirituals "The Lord's Prayer" and "The Virgin Mary had a Baby Boy," both from Trinidad in the time of slavery in the early nineteenth century. After working in the sugar cane fields, the slaves would sing "The Lord's Prayer." It is interesting that the refrain throughout is "Hallowed be Thy name." They recognized that the deepest thing that mattered was that God's name, his power of being, should receive their total commitment, just as he had totally committed himself to them in Christ incarnate, crucified, and risen. The refrain of "The Virgin Mary had a Baby Boy" is:

> He came from the glory,
> He came from the glorious kingdom.
> Oh, yes, believer,
> He came from the glory,
> He came from the glorious kingdom.

Our people have understood from experience the humiliation of the birth of Christ. He was poor, vulnerable, and exposed to oppression by Herod. We have known all about the Herods of this world. But our people grasped that this weak, poor, exposed babe of Bethlehem came from the glorious kingdom. His true existence was from and in God. Indeed, God was present in the cradle. In the end, God's power is made perfect in weakness. This was not a theological dictum, but a conviction from the depths of our experience of God within our experience of life. That is why we have not only survived as a people but survived with grit and gaiety.

As a typical Caribbean man, I am made up of various cultural heritages — Carib, African, Irish, French — and therefore with a universal tendency. Early I developed a passion for history and geography. It is therefore no surprise that experiencing God for me means experiencing his varied grace and wisdom. Experiencing God in the dialogue between cultures is part of my own inner and outer experience and therefore constitutes my calling. Happily, during more than thirty years in the ecumenical movement I have had the privilege of carrying out this calling in an extraordinary variety of ways.

\* \* \*

As I said, the Caribbean was the testing ground of what was to be the experience of Asians, Latin Americans, and black people in North America and Africa. This comes out particularly in the history of the experiences of God which underlie the development of black theology in the USA. In part it has been stimulated by the writings and activities of Caribbean activists, among them Edward Blyden, Marcus Garvey, George Padmore, Aimé Césaire, Frantz Fanon, Malcolm X, and Stokely Carmichael. These men contributed greatly to the development of Black Power in the USA and African personality or *négritude* in Africa.

Perhaps the best-known exponent of black theology in the USA is James Cone. Let me say immediately that our experience in the Caribbean is nothing compared with that of our black brothers and sisters in the USA. We were liberated, after a mixture of rebellion and enlightened self-interest and good sense, in 1834. Having drained the wealth of the Caribbean, the colonial powers became more interested in Asia and later Africa. We were left pretty much on our own, freed in body if not in spirit. This has not been so for American blacks. In the land of the free, blacks were excluded, oppressed, denigrated — and still are, even if it is now illegal to do so. Yet they have had a rich experience of God, immortalized in the spirituals. Cone puts the matter clearly in *God of the Oppressed*:

> Like white American theology, black thought on Christianity has been influenced by its social context. But unlike white theologians, who spoke to and for the culture of the ruling class, black people's religious ideas were shaped by the cultural and political existence of the victims in North America. Unlike Europeans who immigrated

to this land to escape from tyranny, Africans came in chains to serve a nation of tyrants. It was the slave experience that shaped our idea of this land. And this difference in social existence between Europeans and Africans must be recognized, if we are to understand correctly the contrast in the form and content of black and white theology.

What then is the form and content of black religious thought when viewed in the light of their social situation? Briefly, the form of black religious thought is expressed in the style of story and its content is liberation. Black Theology, then, is the story of black people's struggle for liberation in an extreme situation of oppression. Consequently there is no sharp distinction between thought and practice, worship and theology, because black theological reflections about God occurred in the black struggle of freedom.

The astonishing thing about the black American experience is that it was their experience of God which sustained them when they were being oppressed by those who claimed to believe in the same God. Black Americans embraced the realism of the Scriptures, and found that, in spite of appearances to the contrary, God as revealed in Christ was one who could be trusted, one who affirmed their humanity, whose promises were sure not only beyond this life, but within it. The spirituals are witnesses to this triumphant faith. In *The Spirituals and the Blues*, Cone writes:

> The divine liberation of the oppressed from slavery is the central theological concept in the black spirituals. These songs show that black slaves did not believe that human servitude was reconcilable with their African past and their knowledge of the Christian gospel. They did not believe that God created Africans to be the slaves of Americans. Accordingly they sang of a God who was involved in history — their history — making right what whites had made wrong. Just as God delivered the Children of Israel from Egyptian slavery, drowning Pharaoh and his army in the Red Sea, he will also deliver black people from American slavery. It is this certainty that informs the thought of the black spirituals, enabling black slaves to sing:
>
> Oh Mary, don't you weep, don't you moan,
> Oh Mary, don't you weep, don't you moan,
> Pharaoh's army got drownded,
> Oh Mary, don't you weep.
>
> The basic idea of the spirituals is that slavery contradicts God; it is a denial of his will. To be enslaved is to be declared nobody, and

that form of existence contradicts God's creation of people to be his children. Because black people believed that they were God's children, they affirmed their somebodiness, refusing to reconcile their servitude with divine revelation....

The message of liberation in the spirituals is based on the biblical contention that God's righteousness is revealed in his deliverance of the oppressed from the shackles of human bondage. That message was an expression of the slave's confidence that God can be trusted to do what he said he would. God does not lie.... The faith of black people was thus grounded in the authenticity of God's Word revealed through the scriptures.

Even when nothing seemed to change around them, the blacks continued to sing:

> God is a God!
> God don't never change!
> God is a God
> And He always will be God.

How strangely this sounds when we remember Luther's exclamation: "Let God be God!" But Luther himself could not come to terms with the challenge of the peasants with the same cry on their suffering lips.

The black Americans were never parochial in their experience of God or in their expression of it. If God is truly God, then he is God of all humanity. Their experience was, in the deepest sense, ecumenical. One of my favourite spirituals is "He's got the whole world in his hands," and I can never forget hearing Marian Anderson singing it:

> He's got the whole world in his hands;
> He's got the big round world in his hands;
> He's got the wide world in his hands;
> He's got the whole world in his hands.
>
> He's got you and me, Brother, in his hands;
> He's got you and me right in his hands;
> He's got you and me, Sister, in his hands;
> He's got the whole world in his hands.
>
> He's got ev'rybody in his hands;
> He's got ev'rybody in his hands;
> He's got ev'rybody in his hands;
> He's got the whole world in his hands!

Martin Luther King caught that vision. As Cone says in *God of the Oppressed*:

> King's creative thought and power in the struggle of freedom were found in his black Church heritage. This was the heritage that brought him face to face with agony and despair but also hope and joy that somewhere in the bosom of God's eternity, justice would become a reality "in the land of the free and the home of the brave." This was the source of King's dream and his anticipation that "trouble won't last always." With black sermonic style and rhythm and with theological imagination, he attempted to explicate the content of his vision: "I have a dream," he said at the March on Washington in 1963, "that one day my children will no longer be judged by the color of their skin but by the content of their character." And the night before his assassination in Memphis, he reiterated a similar hope: "I may not get there with you, but I want you to know tonight that we as a people will get to the promised land." The idea that hope is created in the context of despair and oppression is what made King such a creative activist and a great preacher.

But King did not stop there. He related the struggle of the American blacks with that of the Vietnamese against American military aggression. He championed the cause of oppressed people everywhere. In his last Christmas sermon in 1967 he said:

> I have a dream that one day men will rise up and come to see that they are made to live together as brothers....
>
> I still have a dream today that one day war will come to an end....
>
> I still have a dream that with this faith we will be able to adjourn the councils of despair and bring new light into the dark chambers of pessimism. With this faith we will be able to speed up the day when there will be peace on earth and goodwill toward men. It will be a glorious day, the morning stars will sing together, and the sons of God will shout for joy.

He gave his life for that dream — in living hope.

When we sing the spirituals and the blues, when we listen or dance to jazz, let us never forget that they are expressions of American blacks' experience of God — and in the process they have enriched our humanity.

\* \* \*

To speak of experiencing God in Africa is a daunting task. Africa is so vast, so impenetrable, so tempestuous in its vitality, so devastating in its disasters. Africa has as many cultures as it has languages, and that means hundreds. For a long time, those who saw all the light coming from Europe called Africa the dark continent, but the light in this case was one that blinded and consumed rather than illuminated. Yet the light of the gospel has shone in Africa. The astonishing thing is that, in spite of all its associations with Western imperialism, the Christian faith has been welcomed by millions of Africans; and some have predicted that by the end of this century there will be more Christians in Africa than on any other continent.

Recent African writers have reminded us that for centuries there has been a deep sense of a supreme God as Creator, Father, Protector, the Great Spirit. John Mbiti, who has collected a great deal of material about this in his books, sums up the picture of God which emerges from African prayer:

> It shows him to be personal, approachable, loving, kind, giver and preserver of life, and the Father who creates all things. In praying to God, people's attitudes are summed up in the words of one prayer: "Oh God of our forefathers, all our lives depend on you and without you we are nothing" (*The Prayers of African Religion*).

The Christian gospel came to fertile soil in Africa. But in the mind of those who brought Christianity there were many thorns and much stony ground. Polygamy, veneration of ancestors, traditional medicine, strange rituals, ecstatic dancing, tribalism — these were seen as stumbling-blocks to a Christianity with a European dress. And African Christians have been required to put on that dress. But thanks to the work of anthropologists, sociologists, and historians, African theologians are beginning to bring out the rich and varied cultural context within which God in Christ is experienced. New insights are being uncovered, especially by the African independent churches. Here we can only mention a few:

(1) There is a profound sense of the relation between creation, nature, and human beings. In Africa, nature and the animal world are more often cruel than benevolent. And yet, human beings master them not in order to dominate and

despoil them, but to make them friendly and serviceable for the well-being of all. Africans instinctively understand what Paul is talking about in Romans 8 :18-27 when he speaks of creation as waiting for its liberation by the children of God.

(2) Africans have a keen sense of sight. "Seeing God" and seeing one's fellow human being are intimately related. Nowhere else have I known my humanity to be so deeply proved, challenged, and affirmed as in Africa when a village man or woman has seen through me. And the wonderful smile which breaks out from the eyes and face when that affirmation is reciprocated! John Taylor, in his perceptive book *The Primal Vision*, tells of a young Ugandan girl who sat with him in a village hut as he busied himself about. She said nothing, just sat quietly. Then she got up and said goodbye in the words of her language: "I have seen you." A Bushman prays to God for immortality: "Take my face and give me yours." Experiencing the God of Abraham, Isaac, and Jacob, the God of the prophets, and above all the God of our Lord Jesus Christ in Africa can be a marvelous witness to that sense of sight, expressing the inner reality of our humanity as made in God's image.

(3) The African experience of God is never individualistic, never something to be enjoyed only for and by oneself. The individual is a person in community, and that community includes the living and the dead. The communion of the saints can and will become a living reality. The rich treasure of African proverbs and sayings, summing up the aphoristic wisdom of the ages, testifies to this. The best way to understanding this facet of the African experience of God is to read the novels and poetry of Africans.

These are only three brief hints of what experiencing God in Africa can mean. The Independent Churches are by no means sentimental about these religious traditions. While some scholars, even theologians, talk about returning to African traditions, these churches judge everything in African religious tradition which is clearly contrary to God's word and challenge the traditions to make them obedient to Christ. But they are also discovering much in the biblical tradition that enables them to explore their own traditions — prayer, fasting, dreams, ecstasies, angels, healing, sharing in community, the communion of the saints, and the coming again of Christ in glory — elements being explored in Western Christianity today largely by the charismatic renewal. What the Africans are asserting is the nearness of God and his power in Christ to save, to heal, to give assurance, hope, and life to all.

\* \* \*

In the years following its discovery by Europeans, Latin America had much the same experience as the Caribbean. Today the Latin American experience of God is described in terms of liberation, and a lively theology of liberation has emerged. Latin American Christianity has been predominantly Roman Catholic for over 400 years; Anglo-Saxon and German Protestantism are just over a century old there. In either case, the way Latin Americans have until recently experienced God has been very Western. The population is mostly European in its origins, the indigenous Indians having been annihilated, assimilated, or just pushed into a corner. Latin America has experienced the deepest contradictions of Western civilization and has been the field of Western imperialism in the most uninhibited way. In this situation the question of God has become a burning issue.

Among the many Latin American Christians who have reflected profoundly on this situation is Juan Luis Segundo. Volume III of the remarkable book in five volumes, *A Theology for Artisans of a New Humanity*, treats *Our Idea of God*. Segundo describes the crisis Latin Americans face as they break the identity of the West and Christianity:

> It is easy enough to see the tension produced by this situation in Christian consciousness, particularly with respect to the image of God. On the one hand, once the capitalist system has revealed the full dimensions of its inhuman domination in the course of its development, the Christian finds no element in his concrete societal existence that would help him to ponder the God who revealed himself in Jesus Christ. What is more, his indictment of the social system necessarily leads him to criticize a notion of God which is the projection of the false image created by an ideology of domination. In this sense we can say that never before has it been so difficult to conceive the Christian God in real-life terms.
>
> At the same time, however, we see dawning on the horizon the possibility of a new organization of societal life that will overcome

the dominator-versus-dominated dialectic. This fact bespeaks the dawning of a new, more profound, more authentic image of God. So we can also say that never before, even in the West, have we been so close to discovering the true face of God.

Experiencing God today in Latin America means hearing again the voice of God in the cries of the poor, the oppressed, the marginalized millions. It is hearing again the word of God through the prophets and in the life and ministry of Jesus. It is coming to grips through our lives with the institutional violence and domination which exist in each country, backed by the economic, military, and political involvement of the rich nations. As Segundo has written:

> The more we are conscious of the oppressive forces and structures of society over our minds, the more we become able to understand the word of God concealed by these forces. And the more we understand the liberating word of God in human history, the more we are confronted with inhuman and unjust structures in our societies.

Experiencing God is therefore born in a clear-eyed, intelligent, committed involvement in the struggle for liberation while listening again to the clear biblical message of God as the Saviour, Liberator. Listen to Ernesto Cardenal, the Nicaraguan priest, poet, mystic, and political activist, as he speaks in the language of Psalm 130:

> From the depths, I cry to you oh Lord!
> I cry in the night from the prison cell
> and from the concentration camp
> From the torture chamber
> in the hour of darkness
> hear my voice
>      my S.O.S.

> If you were to keep a record of sins
> Lord, who would be blameless?
> But you do pardon sins
> you are not implacable as they are in their Investigation!

> I trust in the Lord and not in leaders
> Nor in slogans
> I trust in the Lord and not in their radios!

My soul hopes in the Lord
more than the sentinels of dawn
more than the way one counts the hours of night in a prison cell.

While we are imprisoned
　　　they are enjoying themselves!
But the Lord is liberation
the freedom of Israel.

Latin Americans pose uncomfortable questions to Europeans and North Americans. Can there be a dialogue between Christians of Latin America and those of Europe and North America when the latter are the conscious or unconscious partners of the oppressors? Which God are we really experiencing — the God of the Bible or a God who is masked by our economic and social structures?

To experience God as Liberator of the poor and the oppressed within their struggle is to bear the cross — to be imprisoned, tortured, assassinated. But it is also to experience the living God, who is breaking up the powers of death and darkness and bearing new life and light. To experience God in his battle with rebellious history is the recreative act, the act of Christ in restoring by love God's image in human beings.

\* \* \*

Asian religious thought and practice have always had a great fascination for Westerners. For a number of years yoga and Transcendental Meditation have been fashionable among Europeans and North Americans seeking to slake their spiritual thirst. Hindu and Buddhist missions to the West respond to the hunger of Westerners for self-fulfilment and wholeness of being. An encounter with other faiths is thus forced on us in the West, though we are still reluctant to come to terms with it. Christians in Asia, on the other hand, form a tiny minority among the teeming millions who are seeking to experience God in their many ways. Their challenge is to show in an authentically Asian way — and that in turn may mean different things in different countries of the world's most populous continent — how God is experienced and proclaimed as revealed in Christ.

But Asia is not only the continent of the great religions of the world. It is another area which has been through the experience of the economic and political dominance of the West. For the last thirty years it has been going through a great upheaval and awakening. Millions of peasants are no longer willing to accept their fate of poverty and early death as their only release from it. Amid the tragic contradictions of corrupted wealth and oppressive poverty in most Asian countries, the same forces which are at work in Latin America, the Caribbean, and Africa are also operating. The cry for liberation and for a God who makes people truly human is heard there too. But the Asian cultural context is quite different from the other areas of the Third World, and so the experience of God is expressed in different ways.

From among the many illustrations of how Asian Christians are experiencing God, let me select only two examples — India and Japan. In India the Hindu search for inner unity is pervasive. Human existence is seen in terms of its many contradictions — life/death; spirit/matter; health/sickness. The task is to discover the self hidden within one which is identical with the Self of the Universe, "I am It." This is what lies at the root of yoga and similar practices. There is no external authority over one, either of scriptures or of religious institutions. The only authority which matters is experience (*anubhava*), which is the inner vision of reality which resolves the contradictions and grasps the human being in his totality (*dristi*). What then about the suffering millions on the margin of existence, who do not have the energy or time to indulge in such experiences? Rabindranath Tagore was very painfully aware of this. In *Towards Spiritual Man*, he wrote:

> However unpleasant it may be, we must admit that neither the capacity nor the effort to bear the sorrows of others, intrinsic in the love of God, is widely evident in our country.... We have sought the delights of divine love to the exclusion of its pain.... There is no spirituality in the cultivation of suffering for some ultimate gain; true spirituality lies in suffering for the sake of love....

In the face of this challenge, Indians have come to experience God in the Christ who came as reality incarnate, who took on himself the sufferings of humanity and brought a new creation into being, a new resolution of the contradictions through his death and resurrection. Paul Devanandan speaks for many Indians when he writes:

> Christians believe that with the coming of Christ, God Almighty identified Himself for a while with man in all man's struggles for perfection and the realisation of his true nature. Such identification initiates a new era in creation. It marked the beginning of a redemptive movement, which takes humanity in its entirety, that is the whole community of mankind inclusive of all peoples, whatever their beliefs, language or race. So that, far from shutting others out from participation (which would be being exclusive), the Christian wants to share his faith in this all-inclusive cosmic process of a new creation.

In Japan, as we mentioned in an earlier part of this chapter, Christians have been experiencing God in terms of the pain of God. Not only does this relate to events of twentieth-century history — the Japanese imperialistic aggression in Asia or the devastation wrought by the atomic bombs dropped on Hiroshima and Nagasaki. Much more it is a response to an age-old understanding of life. An early Buddhist scripture expounds the "Noble Truth of Suffering": "Birth is painful; old age is painful; sickness is painful; death is painful; grief, lamentation, pain, dejection, despair, are painful; the wish which one does not obtain — that, too, is painful." To be a self-conscious person is to be in a state of suffering. Therefore the task is to undergo a process of self-culture, "the Noble Eight-fold Path," to overcome pain and to do so without the intervention of some divine being.

Kazoh Kitamori's pioneering book *The Pain of God*, to which we alluded earlier, was deeply influenced by Luther's writings. But reading the Reformer threw Kitamori back to the source he and Luther had in common — the word of God — and to the challenges of his culture and of the historical situation in Japan in the 1930s and 1940s. He came to see the whole meaning of God's revelation in history as God in pain, with his seeking love reaching out to all his creatures, so that through him they may come to life in all its fullness. At the end of the book Kitamori writes:

> My prayer night and day is that the gospel of love rooted in the pain of God may become real to all men. All human emptiness will be filled if this gospel is known to every creature, since the answer

to every human problem lies in the gospel. Therefore I pray, "May thou, O Lord, make known to all men thy love rooted in the pain of God." The greatest joy and thanksgiving comes from the knowledge that this prayer is being granted and that step by step this gospel is becoming real to mankind.

## Toward a universal dialogue of cultures

The sampling we have just taken of the experience of God in various cultures other than those of the North Atlantic has revealed nothing esoteric. Indeed, what strikes one is how all of these experiences — and many others which we have not had space to describe — go to the heart of God's own revelation of himself in history, culminating in the coming, death, and resurrection of Jesus Christ. All of them take with radical seriousness the truth of the word of God, and they do so out of the white heat of participation in the struggle of their people for a more just and authentic existence.

Neither the experience of God nor that reflection on this experience which constitutes doing theology can be genuine if we are not engaged with our whole being in the work of God in our particular culture, with and for other human beings, who bear his image. Only in such a dialogue will the many-sided grace and wisdom of God be revealed, that grace and wisdom which lead to life in all its fullness.

But there is also a dialogue beyond the one with our own culture, a dialogue which has been taking on increasing importance in our shrinking world. The ecumenical movement in recent years has placed greater emphasis on the unity of humanity as an essential element of its task. This quest for the unity of humankind is seen as the struggle for a just society, in which barriers of class, race, and sex are broken down, divisions of peoples and nations are reconciled in peace, and the environment is made sustainable for the well-being of all. Now, thanks to the theological insights coming from around the world and tested in dialogue with people of living faiths and ideologies, there is another dimension of the ecumenical vision which demands our attention. I would call it the universal dialogue of cultures.

It is strange that although *oikoumene* means the whole inhabited earth — humanity — we have given little attention to what this community of peoples in all their variety of cultures could mean in ecumenical perspective. What is the Christian vision of such a community? Perhaps this blind spot is not so strange when we realize that for the past four or five centuries the *oikoumene* has been seen in Western terms. In the Roman Empire the *oikoumene* signified the so-called civilized world, in other words, that part of the world which was under Roman sway. Other countries, peoples, and cultures were regarded as barbarian. Similarly, there is an enduring tendency to regard Western civilization, which some still call Christian, as the norm of what the *oikoumene* should be, despite the events of forty years which have shattered this limited vision, based on military, economic, and political power achieved through scientific and technological progress.

Roger Garaudy, the well-known French Marxist thinker, refers to this dominance by the West as an "accident" in two senses. First, in the time span of human history, Western dominance is of short duration. Second, it has been a disaster both for the West and for the rest of the world, distorting or destroying much that was precious in people's relations with nature, society, and the supernatural. The only way to recover the dimensions of the human developed in all the cultures of the world is through a universal dialogue of cultures. Let us follow this cue and see what it yields in terms of the Christian ecumenical vision.

Early in the Letter to the Hebrews the writer declares: "For it was not to angels that God subjugated the *oikoumene* to come, of which we are speaking" (2:5). Already the writer has referred to the incarnation in terms of bringing or presenting the first-born to the *oikoumene* (1:6), whom the angels are summoned to worship. The *oikoumene* to come, the new order of humanity, is evoked by the words of the Psalmist:

What is man that thou art mindful of him,
or the son of man, that thou carest for him?
Thou didst make him for a little while lower than the angels,
thou hast crowned him with glory and honour,
putting everything in subjection under his feet
(2:6-8, quoting Psalm 8:4-6).

Humanity was created by God to share his glory and honour, his manifest being, and to bring the whole creation into the sphere of that being, God's purpose of good. The writer goes on to declare that it is Jesus who has fulfilled the vision of the Psalmist. He it is who is "crowned with glory and honour because of the suffering of death, so that by the grace of God he might taste death for every one. For it was fitting that he, for whom and by whom all things exist, in bringing many persons to glory, should make the pioneer of their salvation perfect through suffering" (Heb. 2:9-10). What the writer is saying is that something radically wrong has happened to the present *oikoumene.* It has failed to live up to the purpose of God and has rebelled against him. The one thing which has *oikoumene* in its grip is the fear of death, the fear of its annihilation. Where God's life, his glory and honour, has been refused, there death reigns.

But Jesus is the pioneer of the salvation of the *oikoumene.* Already the writer has spoken of the angels as servants of those who are to obtain salvation (1:14), and we are asked how we can escape a just retribution if we neglect such a great salvation as is offered in this Jesus, he who saves (2:3). As we saw in the first chapter, the biblical meaning of "salvation" points to breadth and wholeness and liberation in this life. The human being who has received salvation is one who is truly and authentically himself or herself. What the Letter to the Hebrews is saying is that the *oikoumene* to come, the new humanity, is already manifest in Jesus, he who saves, he who is himself authentic, integral, whole, human as we are destined to be. He is the pioneer, the representative of this coming *oikoumene,* and we become part of it when we see Jesus and follow his pioneering representative steps.

At the end of Hebrews, the writer describes the coming *oikoumene* as "the city to come," reminding us that the Greeks often substituted *oikoumene* for *polis*:

> For we have no lasting city, but we seek the city which is to come. Through him then let us continually offer up a sacrifice of praise to God, that is, the fruit of lips that acknowledge his name. Do not neglect to do good and to share what you have, for such sacrifices are pleasing to God (Heb. 13:14-16).

Earlier he declares more explicitly, "You have come to Mount Zion and to the city of the living God, the heavenly Jerusalem" (12:22). It is important to note that the life in this city is a sacrifice, an offering of praising God, doing good, and sharing what we have. The true life of the *oikoumene*, the *polis*, is this offering of the self to our Creator and sharing our selves with each other. That is what it means to be truly human. The Revelation to John completes the picture of this *polis*, this new Jerusalem, this new heaven and earth, this *oikoumene* to come (Rev. 21-22).

To understand this vision of the city as the symbol of the fulfilment of history, we must again turn back to the story of Babel (Gen. 11:1-9), where people tried to build a city going up to heaven to ensure that they would not be scattered all over the earth and also to make a name for themselves. The unity of humanity was regarded as humanity making a name for itself over against God. Challenging this act, God says: "This is only the beginning of what they will do: and nothing that they propose to do will be impossible for them" (Gen. 11:6) — a marvelous description of what was already a fact of history. The inner character of empires and powerful states is to unify peoples under their domination, to homogenize nations into one culture, one language, one style of living under one human power. So God punishes the people and at the same time reasserts his plan that there be many nations as a sign of the manifold character of his creative purpose.

But the punishment is soon turned into a promise. In the next chapter God calls Abram out of his home and culture in Ur of the Chaldees and promises him, "In you all the families of the earth will be blessed" (Gen. 12:3). All the families of the earth will, by their faith-commitment to this God, be enabled to share their rich variety of cultures, languages, and identities with one another.

It is therefore not surprising that Revelation takes up the human story of the building of the city and shows how God deals with the varied nations and cultures of the *oikoumene*. Babel means "gate of God." The original gate would have been one into which all peoples were forced as a manifestation of imperial ambitions. The walls of the city in Revelation are adorned with precious stones of every kind. Its gates are always open to all and it is full of light, the light of the Lord God

Almighty and of the Lamb, the Jesus who tasted death for every one. "By its light shall the nations walk and the kings of the earth shall bring their glory into it.... They shall bring into it the glory and the honour of the nations" (Rev. 21 :18-26).

Moreover, they will be turned to God and to the Lamb, "and they shall see his face and his name shall be on their foreheads" (Rev. 22:4). They will bear his name, his inner character of sacrificial love, rather than assert and impose their name over others. Their true being will be in God, and the manifestations of that being will be seen in all their manifold creativity. The *oikoumene* to come, the city to come, is open to all and is full of the variety of the riches of creation, culture, which all the peoples bring. It is the place of the universal dialogue of cultures.

Lewis Mumford, at the end of his long and detailed study of *The City in History*, outlines a similar vision of the city to come:

> The task of the coming city... is to put the highest concerns of man at the centre of all his activities: to unite the scattered fragments of the human personality, turning artificially dismembered men — bureaucrats, specialists, "experts," depersonalized agents — into complete human beings, repairing the damage that has been done by vocational separation, by social segregation, by the over-cultivation of a favoured function, by tribalisms and nationalisms, by the absence of organic partnerships and ideal purposes.... We must now conceive the city, accordingly, not primarily as a place of business or government, but as an essential organ for expressing and actualizing the new human personality — that of "One World Man."

The point is that this universal dialogue of cultures is not a completely new idea which has arisen out of our contemporary situation, in which the peoples and cultures of the world have been brought closer together. It has in fact always been central to the Christian message with its concern for the *oikoumene* to be, that is, the earth becoming a home (*oikos*) in which all are open to each other and can share a common life in all its interweaving variety. Our task is to spell this out in terms of our actual situation today. How do we go about facilitating a universal dialogue of cultures?

"Culture" is of course a notoriously difficult word to define. From its Latin origins, it came to signify three things: (1) the general process of intellectual, spiritual, and aesthetic development, as one engages in tending (*colo, cultus*) creation, the environment; (2) a people's whole way of life including their technology, customs, beliefs, religion, systems of values; and (3) actual works and practices of intellectual and artistic activity. Cicero wrote of "cultivating" the mind or of a "cultured mind." Culture, therefore, has to do with the life of the *oikoumene*, the inhabited earth.

However, strange things happened to this word. In the West there has been a tendency to speak of culture in two ways which are intended to discriminate and exclude. One is to contrast a "cultured" person with an uncultured person, the former being someone well educated and versed in the high arts, over against the masses. The phrase "mass culture" has a very pejorative sense today. More pertinent to our purpose is the tendency to equate culture with civilization and to apply it to the massive power of Western artifacts through science and technology and the particular ways in which the human mind has developed, especially since the invention of printing and other modern communications media. Colonialism was in effect people going abroad to set up their own culture and style of life as a counter to that of the surrounding peoples and rapidly acquiring a sense of superiority. The German writer Herder, in his unfinished book *Ideas on the Philosophy of the History of Mankind* (1784-91), attacked the way in which Europeans were subjugating and dominating the peoples of other continents:

> Men of all the quarters of the globe, who have perished over the ages, you have not lived solely to manure the earth with your ashes, so that at the end of time your posterity should be made happy by European culture. The very thought of a superior European culture is a blatant insult to the majesty of Nature.

An important dimension of culture was developed by the Romans. When Cicero and others spoke of the culture of the mind, they were not referring only to the effort to make the earth more habitable and enjoyable. Rather the culture of the mind became the cultivation of taste, discernment, and judgment about how the world should look, how it could be really made fit for humanity, how it could be humanized. It is a political activity, having to do with life among people. As Hannah

Arendt puts it, in a brilliant essay on "The Crisis of Culture" in her book *Between Past and Present*:

> Culture and politics ... belong together because it is not knowledge or truth which is at stake, but rather judgment and decision, the judicious exchange of opinion about the sphere of public life and the common world, and the decision what manner of action is to be taken in it, as well as to how it is to look henceforth, what kind of things are to appear in it.

Lionel Trilling, the noted American literary critic, has written in his collected essays, *Beyond Culture*:

> To make a coherent life, to confront the terrors of the outer and the inner world, to establish the ritual and art, the pieties and duties which make possible the life of the group and the individual — these are culture.

There is a sense in which a person can be truly human and fully himself or herself only if he or she is in tune with the environment or culture. But it is equally true that only if the environment or culture is in accord with the best tendencies of the person can he or she become truly human and truly himself or herself. So we are back at the political character of culture. Trilling writes: "It is no longer possible to think of politics except as the politics of culture, the organisation of human life toward some end or other, towards the modification of sentiments, i.e. the quality of human life."

Culture and the quality of life remind us of God's will for humanity. Through his Spirit God created man, male and female, in his own image, giving them his power and being (blessing them) to be fruitful and replenish the earth and bring it into his purpose of good (Gen. 1:26-31). The prophets understood this culture of creation in all its forms as a political activity, that is, as the conscious awareness that it is based on and expressed by justice and peace. Current ecumenical discussions on human development emphasize this understanding of culture and the quality of life in theological perspective. The Nairobi Assembly of the WCC said:

> The quality of life problem is at root a theological problem. It concerns the nature of humanity as made in the image of God. In the biblical tradition, being human is not dependent upon human achievement or success. Rather, our worth is dependent upon

acceptance by God, in spite of our shortcomings. God wills for us to be his faithful stewards, enjoying and caring for his creation. At the same time, he also wills for us to be his agents, promoting love, peace, harmony, reconciliation, and justice, within individuals, among neighbours, within societies, between nations, and in the cosmos. The basic Christian principle in this regard is faith in God, love towards him and our neighbours, and hope for salvation in Christ through the Holy Spirit.

Our investigation of the meaning of culture has also indicated the importance of its variety. The cultural identity of peoples must be respected if we and they are to be authentic human beings and mutually enriching. The Bangkok conference on Salvation Today asserted that "Culture shapes the human voice that answers the voice of Christ." The Nairobi Assembly spoke in similar terms when it said:

> Jesus Christ does not make copies: he makes originals. We have found this confession of Christ out of our various cultural contexts to be not only a mutually inspiring, but also a mutually corrective exchange. Without this sharing our individual affirmations would gradually become poorer and narrower. We need each other to regain the lost dimensions of confessing Christ and even to discover dimensions unknown to us before. Sharing in this way we are all changed and our cultures are transformed.

The Christian faith is founded on our Lord's incarnation, that "scandal of particularity" by which he came into a given place and culture — Israel. The text of the gospel was communicated within that particular context; the work of redemption was accomplished within that Hebraic culture, thus renewing and enabling it to be the vehicle of Christ's universal Lordship of the world. Our universal dialogue of cultures must therefore be seen in relation to the vision of the *oikoumene*, the city to come, where the riches of the varied cultures of the world will be shared in the light of God's redeeming work in the Lamb and of his purpose of justice and peace.

But what is meant by "dialogue?" Earlier we noted that it must be more than a mere academic exchange. The Greek word as it occurs in the classical writers and later in the Bible has a range of meanings: converse, discuss, confer, negotiate, persuade, investigate, contend with, ponder, consider, reckon, and even balance accounts. It is essentially an activity between persons. The Latin word nearest to it is *conversari,* from which the English "conversation" is derived. But *conversari* has the connotation of turning to another in the sense of living with, having intercourse with, keeping company with someone. It is a relationship. It is interesting that the Authorized Version of the Bible translates the Greek *politeia* (citizenship) by the word "conversation" in Philippians 3 :20. Dialogue is a conversation with our environment, our culture, our fellow human beings, the sharing of life with life in which one is confronted with all the issues of life and culture.

No one has so profoundly enabled us to understand what dialogue is as the Jewish thinker Martin Buber. In his books *I and Thou* and *Between Man and Man,* as well as in his many essays, Buber's purpose is to promote dialogue in its deepest sense. For him real life is meeting. The history of the world is the dialogue between human beings and God. The fundamental fact of human existence is person-with-person dialogue. Where there is no dialogue, no sharing, there is no reality. The basic movement of the life of dialogue is the turning toward the other. The limits of the possibility of dialogue are the limits of awareness.

It is in his lecture on "Hope for this Hour," delivered in New York in 1952, that Buber has spoken most pertinently to our condition. Robert Hutchins had written of the possibility of a Civilization of the Dialogue: "The essence of the Civilization of the Dialogue is communication. The Civilization of the Dialogue presupposes mutual respect and understanding; it does not presuppose agreement." Buber uses this proposal, so congenial to his mind, in order to say a great deal about our present plight in the world and the challenge of the hour. Let me quote briefly from what he says:

> The essential presupposition for this [Civilization of the Dialogue] is that it is necessary to overcome the massive mistrust in others and also in ourselves .... Nothing stands so much in the way of the rise of a Civilization of Dialogue as the demonic power which rules our world, the demony of basic mistrust.... Direct, frank dialogue is becoming ever more difficult and more rare; the abyss between man and man threatens ever more pitilessly to become unbridgeable....

What one calls the creative spirit of men has never been anything other than the address, the cogitative or artistic address, of those called to speak to those really able and prepared to hear. That which is concentrated here is the universal dynamism of dialogue.... Man wishes to be confirmed by man as he who is, and there is genuine confirmation only in mutuality.... There is no salvation save through the renewal of the dialogical relation, and this means, above all, through the overcoming of existential mistrust.

The hope for this hour is "the renewal of dialogical immediacy between men," which will depend on "their unreserved honesty, their good will with its scorn of empty phrases, their courageous personal engagement."

Martin Buber was speaking here directly to the inner meaning of culture, and to what we are seeking to describe as a universal dialogue of cultures as an essential dimension of the ecumenical vision. This understanding of dialogue has in fact been practiced for some time within the ecumenical movement, thanks to courageous pioneering in thought and witness by Asian, especially Indian, theologians. At an international theological consultation at Chiang Mai, Thailand, in April 1977, the participants declared:

> We see dialogue as a fundamental part of our Christian service within community. In dialogue we actively respond to the command "to love God and your neighbour as yourself." As an expression of our love our engagement in dialogue testifies to the love we have experienced in Christ. It is our joyful affirmation of life against chaos, and our participation with all who are allies of life in seeking the provisional goals of a better human community. Thus we soundly reject any idea of "dialogue in community" as a secret weapon in the armoury of an aggressive Christian militancy. We adopt it rather as a means of living out our faith in Christ in service of community with our neighbours.

These words remind us of what Peter said to the churches of Asia Minor: "In your hearts reverence Christ as Lord. Always be prepared to make a defense to anyone who calls you to account for the hope that is in you, yet do it with gentleness and reverence" (1 Pet. 3 :15). We are to show to others the same profound respect and awe that we show to Christ. And with it must be the gentleness which is expressed in caring concern for the other — the willingness to receive as well as to give, to listen as well as to speak. It is this respect and caring, which Christ displayed to us and demands of us, that we must manifest to others. That is the spirit in which we embark on this universal dialogue of cultures.

# 8. A growing community of faith

The vision of a universal dialogue of cultures is a broad and expansive one. Undertaking it with courage and integrity requires far more than curiosity about others or even openness to learning from their experiences. It demands a commitment in which we are ready to pose difficult questions to ourselves, to have others put difficult questions to us — and to stay around for the answers, despite the threats these answers may raise for our comfortable lives and theologies.

One of the most important resources for undertaking this in the ecumenical movement is captured in that familiar phrase of the Apostles Creed — "the communion of saints." The Basis of the World Council of Churches affirms that the Council is a fellowship of churches, a community or communion of churches which seek to fulfil their common calling. That is, we are a *community* of believers called in *common* to *communicate* with each other and with the world in *communion* with the triune God.

Those four key words derive from Latin roots which mean to bind together, to strengthen and support, to serve and give. Behind them is the conviction that human beings are bound together in the bundle of life. They live from, with, and for each other, and they have obligations to each other in mutual sharing. They have to strengthen and support each other from all that may threaten or deny their life together. The corresponding Greek words are *koinos* and *koinonia*. Among the ancient Greeks, *koinos*, common, had the sense of what concerns all rather than only the individual. The Greeks believed that the individual could only exist in so far as he or she was bound to the whole community. Greek social philosophers used the word *koinos* in speaking of the need for common ownership of property and shared values and ideas. The great sin was *pleonexia*, the attitude and act of annexing more, claiming more for oneself at the expense of others, being grasping, greedy, arrogant, covetous. *Koinonia* meant therefore sharing, participation, friendship, companionship, community, communion. For example, marriage was described as the *koinonia* of the whole life. *Koinonia* was also conceived as the basis of *soteria*, salvation, liberation, the preservation and fulfilment not only of persons but of the whole cosmos.

Of course, these noble ideas and longings were hardly carried out in practice among the Greeks. But they do show that human beings have long had the same perceptions and aspirations as we have today. Political analysts, statesmen, journalists, and church leaders today speak and write a great deal about our pilgrimage toward the year 2000. The vast majority of humankind — the poor, the weak, the oppressed, the marginalized — are expressing themselves too, but through their cries of anguish, their anger, and their actions. All echo what the Greeks and Romans said, although they speak far more of lack of a common life and of community in our world, of the threats to peace and our mutual well-being, and specifically of the *pleonexia*, the grasping avarice which dominates human existence at every level everywhere. That is the human condition, the context in which the church lives and must proclaim the gospel of the kingdom of God and his justice, the challenge of the universal dialogue of cultures, the promise of life in all its fullness.

At the centre of our faith is the message of the kingdom of God, the kingly rule of God over humanity and the whole creation. Our faith affirms that there can be no community, no life in common, no real communication unless our existence is ruled, directed, and fashioned by God the Father who created us for good and sustains us by his love; by God the Son who took on our humanity in order to demonstrate how we can stop being grasping idiots who turn the world into a madhouse and become truly human, sharing a common life as members of his body, the church; and by God the Holy Spirit, who imparts his rich and varied gifts which enable us to use creation rightly and relate to each other in and for community. The kingdom of

God and *koinonia*, community, communion, a common life, communication are one reality.

The WCC's "Guidelines on Dialogue with People of Living Faiths and Ideologies" describe community in Christ in terms of our communication in the church, our communion with God, our communion in fellowship with all members of the body of Christ through history — across distinction of race, sex, caste, and culture — and a conviction that God in Christ has set us free for communion with all peoples and everything which is made holy by the work of God.

> As Christians we are conscious of a tension between the Christian community as we experience it to be in the world of human communities, and as we believe it in essence to be in the promise of God. The tension is fundamental to our Christian identity. We cannot resolve it, nor should we seek to avoid it. In the heart of this tension we discover the character of the Christian Church as a sign at once of people's need for fuller and deeper community, and of God's promise of a restored human community in Christ....

*Communication*

Essential to the ecumenical community is communication between the churches as they seek to fulfil their common calling. Communication happens as the whole people of God listen to one another, share each other's insights and experiences, and enter into ever wider and deeper relationships for the sake of living and witnessing to the gospel. Community and communication are one, not only linguistically but in fact. There cannot be community without communication — the sharing of life with life in gesture, word, and act; and communication should promote community. An African proverb says, "to speak is to love." But too often what passes for communication in our world is loveless and perversely destructive of community.

A serious problem of communication arose within some member churches during the late 1970s over a number of issues, in particular the actions of the Council through its Programme to Combat Racism. But through a process of consultation on how the churches might be involved in combating racism in the 1980s representatives of churches and of racially oppressed or deprived groups in various countries and continents met and talked constructively together in love. The result has been that churches have gained new insights into the problems of racism and of ethnic minorities in their own countries and into the interconnections of these problems on a global scale. The 1980 world consultation in Noordwijkerhout, Holland, brought these national and regional efforts together. This worldwide process of review marked a turning point in the life of the WCC. Churches have been willing to expose themselves to each other and to the world in one of the most tragic blights on our common humanity which tests our credibility as a community of faith in Christ. The issue now being faced is not only how the World Council as such will respond to the challenge of racism in the 1980s, but rather how the churches themselves will do so in each place and in all places.

But there must be a more intensive and direct encounter between the Council and the member churches. It is my earnest hope that we will engage more actively in communication with the churches in the coming years and that they will consider the Council as an integral part of their life.

*Faith*

The World Council is a community of churches which confess the Lord Jesus Christ as God and Saviour. It is a community of faith. That is what distinguishes it and other world ecumenical bodies from such international organizations as the United Nations. It is faith in the blessed Trinity which determines our community, communication, and our common life. All our studies, consultations, publications, and actions must be judged on this basis. This is equally true of the member churches. A faith which does not make for community is not true to the gospel. A community which does not find its foundation and driving force in faith in God the Creator, Redeemer and Perfector, is a madhouse.

There is an ongoing determined effort in the WCC to grapple with the centralities of our faith. Significantly, this wrestling with the gospel of the kingdom of God has taken place in terms of the search for community: the poor, human struggles, the use and misuse of power have been the matrix within which the churches' witness of the kingdom happens.

For a number of years the WCC's Faith and Order Commission has worked tirelessly on consensus statements about baptism, eucharist, and the ministry. Anyone having some acquaintance with the history of the church knows that what is at stake here is not just an ecclesiological detail. The apostle Paul was at pains to teach the churches that baptism was no merely formal act. It brought about revolutionary changes in the life of believers and in their attitude to others. "Just as the body is one and has many members, and all the members of the body, though many, are one body, so it is with Christ. For by one Spirit we were all baptized into one body — Jews or Greeks, slaves or free — and all were made to drink of one Spirit" (1 Cor. 12:12-13). "For as many of you as were baptized into Christ have put on Christ. There is neither Jew nor Greek, there is neither slave nor free, there is neither male nor female; for you are all one in Christ Jesus" (Gal. 3:27-28). Baptism is a community-creating act.

Similarly, the eucharist is an act in which we have communion with Christ, who gave his body and blood for us that we might give our body and blood for others. It is the celebration and strengthening of community. Paul says that "anyone who eats and drinks without discerning the body eats and drinks judgment upon himself" (1 Cor. 11:29). As we saw, the context in which he wrote these solemn and harsh words was one in which members of the body of Christ were seeking to isolate themselves from or exclude others (1 Cor. 11:17-22).

Finally, the ministry (*diakonia*) must be conceived in terms of a true succession to him who came not to be ministered to but to minister and to give his life as a ransom for many (Mark 10:42-45). The ministries of the church are intended to build up the life of the people of God that they may be witnesses to the world of life in all its fullness, life in community. How can we better discern the work of the Spirit in bestowing gifts of grace (*charismata*) on the people of God so that they may be a living community of grace, self-giving love, within society?

In these three central theological areas, over which so much polemical ink has been spilled during two thousand years of church history, and on account of which so many divisions have threatened the unity of the Body of Christ, Christians committed to the ecumenical movement have worked long and hard to achieve the community necessary to fulfil our common calling.

## Sharing

Community is synonymous with sharing what we are and what we have. The heart of our faith is a God who shared himself in his own triune being of Father, Son, and Holy Spirit and, above all, shared himself with his creation of humanity and nature. The kingdom of God is the reality and promise of this community of sharing in the Godhead. When Paul in 2 Corinthians 8-9 appeals to the factious church of Corinth to share its wealth with the poor mother church of Jerusalem, he uses all the key words of the faith — grace and thanksgiving (*charis*), joy (*chara*), love (*agape*), service (*diakonia*), liturgy (*leiturgia*), equality (*isotes*), blessing (*eulogia*), openhearted generosity (*haplotes*), and communion (*koinonia*). He sums it up by saying: "Under the test of this service, you will glorify God by your obedience in confessing the gospel of Christ, and by the generosity of your contribution (*koinonia*) for them and for all others; while they long for you and pray for you, because of the surpassing grace of God in you. Thanks be to God for his inexpressible gift!" (2 Cor. 9:13-15). Sharing our resources, whatever they are, is a confession of the gospel of Christ and an act of obedience in which we glorify God and contribute to creating and sustaining true community.

A church which aims to be a community of people committed to God and to his purpose will be a church which affirms the mutual interdependence of all its parts, rises above its various national identities and gratefully affirms its universality in Christ, shares decision-making across the world's divisions, dares to confront the powers of this world, be they political, economic, or cultural, and in the name of the crucified Christ, calls for justice for the poor and oppressed.

The willingness of the church to share — even to risk — its resources, in Christ's name and by God's grace, can be a parable for global sharing. In a world in which the language of faith has lost meaning for lack of translation into life, the acting out of God's kind of sharing announces as no words can the good news of Christ to humankind.

One of the challenges to a community of sharing is the relation between women and men in church and society. In the older version of the Genesis creation story we read: "Then the Lord God said, 'It is not good for the man to be alone, I will provide a partner for him'" (Gen. 2:18). This partner comprised all living creatures and supremely woman who became united to him. Man alone would be just an individual without the companionship and support which would help to maintain his existence and create community. Indeed, one of the later prophets, Malachi, when referring to the apostasy of Israel, speaks of the relations of husband and wife: "The Lord has borne witness against you on behalf of the wife of your youth. You have been unfaithful to her, though she is your partner [companion] and your wife by solemn covenant" (2:14). Note that the accent is not on the procreation of children or on all those ideas of subordination which have bedeviled our human story, but rather on companionship, mutual support, community, and communion. It is the primal vision of God's purpose for women and men which has been asserted and explored in the WCC's study and consultations on "The Community of Women and Men in the Church."

## A community of struggle for true human community

It is evident that the churches and the World Council of Churches are very pale manifestations of the community (*koinonia*) the gospel reveals and demands and people throughout the ages have longed for. We are part of what hinders true community, because as part of our broken societies we behave accordingly. As the community of pardoned sinners we are called to participate in the struggles of people for true community, and that includes enabling them to participate in discovering and availing themselves of the sources of and resources for true community. That is why the ecumenical movement has been involved in the issues of human rights, militarism, the arms race and disarmament, and the conflicts of our world. All these issues are interrelated. They are interwoven manifestations of the denial of the kingdom of God and therefore of community.

At Bristol in 1967, the Faith and Order Commission stated: "Unity means reconciliation, and the object of God's reconciling work is the created world. This work of God is the over-coming of the destructive and disruptive forces of rebellion and the effecting of the oneness of all men as they are reconciled and perfected in Christ."

That report went on to ask:

> What is the function of the Church in relation to the unifying purpose of God for the world? What relation does the concept of the Church as institution bear to the concept of the Church as that part of the world which already lives as God's world, i.e. as acknowledging God's judgment, forgiveness and claim to obedience? Does the former concept imply that in the fulfilment of God's reconciling purpose for the world the Church, as institution, is to be discarded, while the latter concept implies the consummation of the Church in terms of the renewal of the created world? What, then, is the relation of the churches' quest for unity among themselves to the hope for the unity of mankind? If such a relation is not determined and maintained, is there danger that the movement towards institutional unity may become a form of escapism?

It was out of these insights and searching questions that the Faith and Order Commission embarked on a study on the unity of the church in its relation to the quest for true human community.

We will therefore not be bullied by those who attack us for giving our attention to controversial political issues either because they claim that it detracts from the proclamation of the gospel and the search for the unity of the church or because they do not wish to be involved out of fear or indifference or a feeling of helplessness. Necessity is laid upon us to witness to the kingdom of God in these conflicts and to be instruments of God's reconciling word and act in Christ. In the midst of the gloom and despair of our time we must use every nerve of wit and will to let God's way be known and followed. In this we will join hands with all who are struggling for peace and justice in the world while we keep our minds firmly and critically centred in God's will and work. And in all this we will deploy what the German evangelist and social reformer Christoph Blumhardt called "the ceaseless prayer for the power of persistence," as those who fervently wait for the promise of the kingdom.

*A community of life and joy*

In this brief survey of our work as a community of communication, of faith, of sharing, and of struggle for true human community, I have singled out some of the things we are involved in as a Council, a community of communities of those who confess the Lord Jesus Christ as God and Saviour. But the work of the Council is really only a small enabling symbol of what is going on in many places.

All over the world there are Christian communities which are signs of life and joy. There are those who dare to challenge the forces of death and despair with the message of the kingdom of God and his justice. These base communities, these people's movements, these charismatic renewal groups, these lay centres, these small experiments in participation in development through self-reliance, these groups working for community health care and seeking to be healing communities, these worshiping congregations creating new songs and new liturgies and supporting one another in a solidarity of faith and witness, these persons who risk or suffer imprisonment, torture, and death for their joyful testimony to God's just rule, these simple, conservative believers who allow their eyes to be opened to the world around them and take the first tentative steps to reach out to their fellow human beings in need — all these are manifestations of the community of life and joy, of the communion of the saints.

They are those who heed the Good Shepherd who lays down his life for his sheep and gives life in all its fullness. They are like the young Christian community in Thessalonica for whom Paul gives thanks because of their work of faith and labour of love and steadfastness of hope in our Lord. They are persons who received the word in much affliction and with joy in the Holy Spirit. Paul exhorts them, as they work and witness in that world of the poor, of slaves, of foreigners, of corrupt oppressors: "Rejoice always, pray constantly, give thanks in all circumstances; for this is the will of God in Christ Jesus for you" (1 Thess. 1:3, 6; 5:16-18).